THE
JOURNEY

A Guide for the Modern Pilgrim

MARÍA RUIZ SCAPERLANDA
MICHAEL SCAPERLANDA

LOYOLAPRESS.

CHICAGO

LOYOLAPRESS.
3441 N. ASHLAND AVENUE
CHICAGO, ILLINOIS 60657
(800) 621-1008
WWW.LOYOLABOOKS.ORG

Cover design by Tracey Harris Sainz
Interior design by Lisa Buckley

Library of Congress Cataloging-in-Publication Data
Scaperlanda, María Ruiz, 1960-
  The journey : a guide for the modern pilgrim / María Ruiz Scaperlanda, Michael Scaperlanda.
    p. cm.
  ISBN 0-8294-1617-X
  1. Spiritual life—Catholic Church. 2. Christian pilgrims and pilgrimages.
I. Scaperlanda, Michael A. II. Title.
BX2350.3.S33 2004
263'.041—dc22

                                                              2004008492

Printed in the United States of America
04 05 06 07 08 09 10 Bang 10 9 8 7 6 5 4 3 2 1

＋∾＋

To our awesome foursome,
Christopher, Anamaría, Rebekah, and Michelle,
who continue to share with us
the lessons of the journey

＋∾＋

Contents

Acknowledgments

Since the beginning of our courtship and marriage, Michael and I have been blessed by the fellowship of many kind teachers, friends, and spiritual companions who have walked with us on our adult pilgrimage. We simply would not be who we are without them.

We want to thank in a special way our parents, Carolyn Ann (who has completed her earthly pilgrimage) and Anthony Scaperlanda, and María de Jesus and Ignacio Ruiz. You toiled and worked the soil of our young hearts, planting the seeds of faith, vision, and discipleship. To you we owe the roots of our spiritual journey as individuals—and the groundwork of who we are as a couple. *Muchas gracias!*

Our four children each contributed to this project in numerous ways. Specifically, thank you Christopher for your prayers as you traveled the United States as part of NET Ministries. Anamaría, Rebekah, and Michelle, thank you for your prayers and for accepting the additional household responsibilities given to you as the book deadline loomed.

Throughout this project, some of our friends adopted the role of "birthing coach," or as St. Paul says, "true yoke-mate" (Phil 4:3)—cheering us locally and across cyberspace as we gave birth to this project. A special word of gratitude goes to Steve Knippenberg, Anne Przykucki, Judy Reilly, Colleen Smith, Pat Stankus, Ken Stephenson, and Murray Tabb.

Many people who heard that we were coauthors joked that, being spouses, we were crazy to do a writing project together. To each of you, thank you! We have no doubt that your worried prayers on our behalf enabled this to be a truly blessed experience.

Finally, we are particularly grateful to Vinita Wright at Loyola Press who originally encouraged us to explore the concept of writing about pilgrimage as a sacramental approach to life. Many thanks to her, Jim Manney, and the rest of the amazing editorial staff at Loyola Press. We remain sincerely grateful for your vision and for the creative ways that you encourage us to listen to our work.

Prelude to the Journey

Michael and I met as undergraduate students at the University of Texas in Austin, getting to know each other and becoming friends through activities at the University Catholic Center. Our first date, in fact, was an evening of "kicker," or country-western dancing, at Austin's Silver Dollar with a group of students from the Catholic Center!

From the beginning, our relationship was based and centered on our desire to live out our Catholic faith. Clearly, our understanding of what this means has changed tremendously over the past two decades. But it is that desire that continues to fuel our marriage and our individual professional lives, Michael's as a law professor at the University of Oklahoma and mine as a freelance journalist and author.

When Pope John Paul II issued an invitation to Catholics throughout the world to go to Rome to celebrate the Jubilee Year 2000, Michael and I took the invitation seriously. Ever since the children were small, we had dreamed of being able to share such a trip as a family at least once in our life. Making a pilgrimage during the Jubilee Year seemed like the perfect opportunity. And so we began plotting, planning, and dissecting the possibility. By Christmas 1999, we were committed. Our primary Santa gifts that year were a backpack for each of the children and an airline ticket for each of us.

Throughout this book, we will return time and again to that Jubilee Year pilgrimage, sharing with you stories of the road. It was the trip of a lifetime. No mishap or misfortune that we remember could ever compare to the blessings we received, as a family and as individuals, from that pilgrimage. Michael taught in the University of Oklahoma College of Law's summer program at Oxford University's Brasenose College, allowing us an extended stay in Europe. Our Jubilee Year pilgrimage began in mid-June in Rome, where we celebrated the Pentecost Vigil Mass with tens of thousands of other pilgrims in St. Peter's Square. We spent the first three weeks of our pilgrimage traveling by train and backpacking our way through Italy, Austria, Switzerland, Germany, the Netherlands, Belgium, and France. This was followed by the five weeks in Oxford, including long weekends exploring southern England, Ireland, and Scotland. Following Oxford, we took the Channel Tunnel once again to continental Europe, then made our way across France to Lourdes and, finally, to northern Spain, where we spent a week with my grandfather's relatives in Santander and the Cantabria region. Michael, Rebekah, Michelle, and I flew home from Madrid in mid-August, while Christopher and Anamaría returned to Italy and Rome for World Youth Day. Did I mention that this was a once-in-a-lifetime pilgrimage?

All our experiences in life are metaphors for our spiritual pilgrimage. We offer this book as a reflection of the pilgrim life. We hope that the specific stories of our pilgrimage experiences, including the Jubilee Year 2000 summer, lead you beyond the trips themselves and into the heart of the pilgrimage that is your life. If you walk away with one thing, we hope that it centers on the reality that pilgrimage is a spiritual journey, an inner process of the heart and spirit. Our prayer for you is that as you walk this journey with us, you will join us in the ongoing discovery of what it means to be a pilgrim journeying toward God, our true home and final destination.

This book itself has been a pilgrimage for Michael and me. It was our first official joint work project. Even after more than two decades living as a couple, we discovered in this process some wonderful and brand-new gifts in each other's insights into what it means to live a pilgrim life.

In order to bring you the personal flavor of our pilgrimage experiences, we decided that it was important to write in the first person, allowing our individual voices to develop the images in each chapter. At the beginning of each chapter, you will see *Michael* or *María* to designate which one of us is speaking. The ideas, the concepts, the development, and the editing of the project, however, belong to both of us, as a couple.

Last year, Michael and I and our good friends Judy and Phil Reilly joined a group of University of Oklahoma students from our university parish for a delightful evening of live music—James Taylor in concert here in Norman. We leave you with a thought and a prayer, both paraphrases of James Taylor's gifted lyrics: The secret of life is enjoying the lovely ride. May this day set you in motion, but above all, may it show you an ocean.

María and Michael Scaperlanda
Feast of Our Lady of Lourdes

1

Recognizing the Urge to Travel

~ MICHAEL ~

I became aware of pilgrimage at an early age. During the 1970–71 school year, when I was ten, our family—Mom, Dad, and six children ages two to ten—lived in the Netherlands while my dad taught economics at Tilburg University. Taking advantage of a year in Europe, we traveled constantly, including a Christmas pilgrimage to Rome, where we got to celebrate Christmas Mass with Pope Paul VI at St. Peter's Basilica.

There were many places to travel in western Europe, and it was difficult to obtain visas for travel behind the Iron Curtain. Nevertheless, Prague, Czechoslovakia, remained an important destination for our family. During our year abroad, we journeyed there to pray to the Christ child at the statue of the Infant Jesus of Prague in the Church of Our Lady of Victory.

The barbed-wire fences loomed on the horizon as we approached the Czechoslovakian border by car. To this day, I vividly recall the guards, alert in their towers, machine guns in hand. Although my parents had had some difficulty securing our visas in advance, I don't remember the entry itself as memorable, at least compared with our exit. As we left the country, our car was thoroughly searched; seats were removed so that the soldiers could satisfy themselves that we were not harboring any disgruntled citizens trying to flee.

A dark-gray cloud hovered stagnantly over Prague during our visit. Drearily, the people of that city tended to their daily tasks. Soviet soldiers kept watch on every street corner. It had been less than three years since the Soviet Union had invaded Czechoslovakia, ending the short-lived "Prague Spring," and the oppression still hung thick in the air.

We had come to this most unlikely of places to celebrate life. Specifically, we had come to give thanks for the lives of my mom and my younger brothers and sisters. My mom nearly died in 1960 at the age of twenty from complications she experienced after delivering me, her first child. Shortly after giving birth, and with her health failing fast, she had been given the last rites by a priest at Seton Hospital in Austin, Texas. Following the tradition of St. Anthony of Padua and St. Teresa of Ávila, prayers were offered to the Holy Child Jesus, and my mom recovered. Several miracles have been attributed to the Infant of Prague over the centuries. Although I don't know if my mom's recovery can be classified as miraculous, it certainly fostered in my parents a continued devotion to the Infant.

When my family was there in 1971, darkness overshadowed Prague because of the Soviet occupation. But a flicker of hope remained, represented by the candles burning in the Church of Our Lady of Victory that day. And the Prague Spring of 1968 eventually resurfaced in the successful "Velvet Revolution" of 1989.

Václav Havel participated in the Prague Spring, was a leader in the Velvet Revolution, and served as president of the post-Communist Czech Republic. In a 1994 speech at Stanford University, he remarked that "the inner workings of all human beings" across time and culture cause people to "feel that they are somehow parts and partakers of the same integral Being." In other words, our "experience of transcendence" could unite us. He understood that the source of "human dignity, freedom, and responsibility" was "man's relationship to that which transcends him." But, he warned, "[g]iven its fatal incorrigibility, humanity probably will have to go through many more Rwandas and Chernobyls before it understands how unbelievably shortsighted a human being can be who has forgotten that he is not God."

Pilgrimage, in part, helps us remember that we are not God or even a god. It also helps us discover and grow closer to the one who is God. These insights brought my family into the darkness of communist Czechoslovakia searching for the light that radiated from the infant Jesus.

Inner Desires and Outward Movement

We humans possess a seemingly insatiable desire to travel. In the year 2000, there were nearly 700 million international tourist arrivals worldwide (World Trade Organization statistics). In that same year, domestic and inter-national travelers spent more than $590 billion on travel in the United States alone (The Travel Industry Association of America). A sense of adventure, a craving for relaxation, and a desire to see and experience the natural and man-made wonders of the world all drive the travel industry, which is among the top three employers in twenty-nine of the fifty U.S. states.

The traveler often has a deep hunger, a sense of longing, a desire to squeeze more out of life. This yearning sometimes rests in the pit of our stomachs as a vague feeling of restlessness. This thirst for exploration and travel is not new. Centuries before recreational travel became a viable option for the middle class, people traveled vicariously through fiction and the tales told by those returning from the journey. Homer's *Odyssey* and Virgil's *Aeneid* provide ancient accounts of wandering protagonists that still capture the imagination today. Even when met with a dose of skepticism, Marco Polo's accounts of Africa and Asia enchanted his European audiences. From *Gulliver's Travels*, to the adventures of Indiana Jones, to Bilbo and Frodo Baggins's journeys through Middle-earth in Tolkien's fantasies, tales of travel spark the imagination and ignite the human spirit's sense of adventure.

The advent of the railroad, the automobile, and the airplane soon changed the face of travel, opening up new vistas for the adventuresome. Writing in 1908, novelist Edith Wharton proclaimed, "The motor-car has restored the romance of travel" (*A Motor-Flight through France*, p. 1). Freed "from all the compulsions and contacts of the railway, the bondage to fixed hours and the beaten track, . . . it has given us back the wonder, the adventure and the novelty which enlivened the way of our posting grandparents" (p. 1). "Above all these recovered pleasures," Wharton felt, "must be ranked the delight of taking a town unawares, stealing on it by back ways and unchronicled paths, and surprising in it some intimate aspect of past time" (p. 1). In her introduction to Wharton's *A Motor-Flight through France*, Mary Suzanne Schriber says:

> The motor-car enabled Edith Wharton to revel in the mystery, adventure, suspense, and discovery of travel—in short, the thrill of travel that informs the prose of *Motor-Flight* itself. . . . Buildings and towns are personified, cast as actors in the great drama of travel: the statue of the Virgin on the church front at Betharram "calls her pilgrims in." . . . Metaphors evoke the pilgrim adventurer, off on a quest in the spring of the year. . . . "How could one resist the call?" To the narrator of *Motor-Flight*, "Every wanderer through the world has these pious pilgrimages to perform." (pp. xxiv–xxv)

Many desires fuel our journeys. Sometimes we travel because we have no choice. Throughout history, people have left home out of necessity as economic, military, or political considerations caused them to uproot their families and seek better living conditions in foreign lands. According to the United Nation's High Commisioner for Refugees (*2001 Statistical Yearbook*), at the dawn of the third millennium there were more than twenty million displaced persons, driven from their homes for reasons beyond their control.

Sometimes we travel because we are called to by faith. For centuries, Christians, Muslims, Hindus, Buddhists, and others have journeyed, often under very difficult conditions, to their sacred places. Christian pilgrims have headed to the Holy Land, Santiago de Compostela, Canterbury, and other sacred sites in search of transformation and healing, or as acts of obedience and penance.

More and more, we travel for leisure and recreation. This has been a widespread phenomenon for only the last century and a half. In *Telling Travels*, Mary Suzanne Schriber notes a 440 percent increase in the number of travel books published in the second half of the nineteenth century as compared with the first half. She also says that by "the late 1840s, 19 percent of the books charged from the New York Society Library by men and 15 percent of those charged by woman were books on travel" (p. xxiv).

As physical beings, we are bounded by time and space. But as spiritual beings, we have a strong desire to transcend these boundaries. The refugee, the pilgrim, and the tourist—each a sojourner—testify to this reality of our existence.

Refugees fleeing a tyrannical regime have no desire to travel. They want stability in their own culture. But, like the Cuban who sets off in shark-infested waters with nothing more than an inner tube, they are willing to leave home and to risk even death to live fully in an environment where they and their families can flourish. Why? What is it in the human soul that provokes them to take such drastic action?

Pilgrims leave home intentionally with an expectation that the physical journey will fuel the spiritual quest. Why? What is it in the human soul that provokes them to seek the transcendent at all, and especially in the material realm of a physical journey?

Tourists travel to rest body, mind, and soul, or to look in awe at the world's natural wonders, or to experience another culture. Why? What is it in the human soul that provokes them to seek rest not only for the body but also for the spirit? What is it that provokes a person to stand in awe of a Hawaiian sunset or the snowcapped peaks of the Rockies? What provokes a desire to connect with other cultures in both the present and the past?

María and I have encountered people who "have it made," with fame, plush houses and cars, and exotic vacations, yet are unhappy. In contrast, some time ago, María visited Haiti and met a remarkable man whose deep happiness radiated from his soul as he sang God's praises. Blind, with his flesh eaten away by leprosy, this resident of the Western Hemisphere's poorest nation was at peace. Despite their divergent paths, the miserable millionaire and the joyful leper have a common core. They both seek meaning in life, and each starts the journey with a deep hunger for completeness. Intuitively, they understand that wholeness will come from something or someone other than themselves.

Their journey is our journey. How shall I live my life? Where will I find meaning? To whom or what shall I attach myself? These ultimate questions penetrate every human heart and unsettle it. Millions attempt to escape such longing through substance abuse, promiscuity, or some form of thrill seeking. A few go so far as to follow anyone who promises the ultimate journey, whether through mass suicide or other cult behaviors.

And yet millions of others surrender to these questions by journeying (spiritually and sometimes physically) to Rome, Jerusalem, Mount Carmel, Mecca, the Ganges River, the Shikoku temples in Japan, and various other places of "sacred wisdom" in search of answers.

An abiding hunger for meaning permeates us, provoking us to seek our origins, purposes, and destinies. And because we are flesh and blood, our seeking takes place partly through movement in the material world. Given that human beings are sensory, experiencing the world through sight, sound, taste, smell, and touch, it should come as no surprise that the desire to travel—to see, hear, taste, smell, and feel another part of the world or another culture—is part of who we are.

It is only natural that our inner journeys manifest themselves in physical ways. We mark birthdays, for instance, by placing candles on a cake, singing a song, and requiring the honoree to extinguish the flames. Catholic faith makes the vital connection between spirit and matter with rich liturgical and other practices—what some have called the "smells and bells." In this, we follow Christ, who was fully man and fully God, incarnate flesh and eternal Word. Incense rising from the altar heightens our awareness of our prayers rising to the Father. Dipping our fingers in the holy water followed by the sign of the cross brings to our minds (if we are paying attention) our baptism, the Trinity, and the Crucifixion. Just as we have pictures of loved ones in our wallets and on our walls at home, our churches are filled with statues or pictures of the loved ones whom we call saints. And, as we sit at Mary's feet and meditate on Christ's birth, life, death, and resurrection, the rosary beads in our hands help focus our minds on the central mysteries of our Christian faith.

Pilgrimage, Sacred and Otherwise

The *Oxford English Dictionary* defines the word *pilgrim* as "a person on a journey; a wayfarer; a traveler; a wanderer; a sojourner." In this broad sense, each of us is on a pilgrimage, from birth to death. This dictionary definition goes on to say that a pilgrim is "[o]ne who journeys (usually a long distance) to some sacred place, as an act of religious devotion." Finding the material answers inadequate, we seek answers in the transcendent, and our pilgrimages intentionally become spiritual quests. These physical manifestations are signs pointing to a deeper reality. The birthday cake and candles point to the inherent dignity and worth of the one whose birth is being celebrated. The wedding ring symbolizes the unity and oneness of the couple. Genuflecting before the tabernacle deepens our sense of gratitude at Christ's enduring presence in our lives. Similarly, a physical pilgrimage to a sacred site is an outward manifestation leading toward a deeper understanding of God and a more profound awareness of his great love for us.

Pilgrimages come in a variety of shapes and sizes and are undertaken for many different reasons. In addition to religious pilgrimages encompassing many of the world's faith traditions, we discovered a variety of nonreligious pilgrimages while surfing the Internet. To celebrate John Lennon's birthday, those so inclined can embark on the "Beatles Pilgrimage Tour to England." The nature lover might be interested in the "Allegany Nature Pilgrimage" or the "Annual Spring Wildflower Pilgrimage." For those steeped in Civil War–era history, the "U.S. Grant Pilgrimage" or the "Natchez Pilgrimage" might be of interest. For those interested in the enduring issues of peace and justice, there is the "International Peace Pilgrimage" and the "Civil Rights Pilgrimage," which reenacts the march from Selma to Montgomery.

We mention these secular pilgrimages for two reasons: to note the myriad ways in which the universal hunger for pilgrimage takes shape in people's lives and to suggest that all (or nearly all) travel can be a source of pilgrimage for those who open themselves up to God's amazing grace during the journey. God can surprise us anywhere, on any kind of pilgrimage, because God searches us out even when we are not looking for God.

The sacred pilgrimage is the journey of those who deliberately seek answers to the questions of meaning, purpose, and eternity. Instead of seeking fulfillment in things that will never satisfy, the sacred pilgrim sets out to find that which the heart truly desires: God's very presence. The entry for "pilgrimages" in the *Catholic Encyclopedia* explains the practice of marking the spiritual quest with a physical journey as an "instinctive notion of the human heart" and goes on to say:

> The Incarnation was bound inevitably to draw men across Europe to visit the Holy Places, for the custom itself arises spontaneously from the heart. . . . The Egyptians journeyed to Sekket's shrine at Bubastis or to Ammon's oracle at Thebes; the Greeks sought for counsel from Apollo at Delphi and for cures from Asclepius at Epidaurus; the Mexicans gathered at the huge temple of Quetzal; the Peruvians massed in sun-worship at Cuzco and the Bolivians in Titicaca. But it is evident that the religions which centered round a single character, be he god or prophet, would be the most famous for their pilgrimages . . . owing to the perfectly natural wish to visit spots made holy by the birth, life, or death of the god or prophet. Hence Buddhism and Mohammedanism are especially famous in inculcating this method of devotion.

This book explores pilgrimage, which connects the inner yearning with the external journey, from an expressly Catholic perspective. Pilgrimages to sacred sites began very early in Christianity. Eusebius's history of the church recounts that Bishop Alexander made a pilgrimage from Cappadocia to Jerusalem in 217 a.d. According to the Catholic Encyclopedia (under "pilgrimages"), a fourth-century letter by Sts. Paula and Eustochium notes the universality of pilgrimages to Palestine, which date from apostolic times. Through a series of stories from our own experiences, together with a dose of practical suggestions, we invite the reader to join this rich Catholic tradition by intentionally linking the interior spiritual journey toward God with the physical journey through this earthly existence.

Earlier, we contrasted the refugee, the tourist, and the pilgrim. Yet we suggest that pilgrims will carry elements of the refugee and the tourist with them in their travels.

Like the recreational traveler, the pilgrim might want to take in the sights, sounds, and culture of the destination. Pilgrims to Rome, for example, will probably want to see the Vatican Museum, the Roman Forum, and the Trevi Fountain, in addition to the specifically sacred sites. They also might enjoy eating pasta or pizza while sipping wine at a trattoria's outdoor table as the abundant nightlife strolls through Piazza Navona. And, for ice-cream lovers, the trip would seem incomplete without experiencing the heavenly tastes of Italy's gelato.

Like the refugee, the pilgrim will want to approach the journey in a spirit of poverty and dependence. Life's circumstances force refugees to leave behind all they have known and to journey, both physically and spiritually, into an unknown future totally dependent on God and the gifts he bestows along the way. Refugees stand naked before God, either pleading for his mercy or resting, like María's Haitian acquaintance, in his loving arms. Pilgrims consciously decide to present themselves to the Lord, acknowledging their utter dependence on God, with

2

Developing a Pilgrim Heart

~ María ~

I thought I would make a critical, emotional connection when I first saw the province of coffee and tobacco. I thought it would happen when I finally met relatives whom I had known only as a toddler and remembered through my parents' memories. I honestly believed that my heart and spirit would be filled with overwhelming emotion when I looked with my own eyes at the sites of my early life—the home where I lived as a newborn; the cathedral where I was baptized; the park where my parents took me as a toddler to play.

It seemed strange, then, that the most emotional moment of my return to Cuba as a grown woman, after thirty-six years, took place not in my hometown of Pinar del Río but on a Sunday morning while I was standing in Havana's Plaza de la Revolución, or Plaza José Martí as it was known before Fidel Castro.

On that warm and sunny January morning, I was one of hundreds of thousands celebrating Mass with Pope

John Paul II on the final day of his historic visit to the Caribbean island. Yet that morning I stood there as a Cuban, not as a visitor or a tourist or a journalist. In some mystical, indescribable way, these were my people. And still the reality was that I was simultaneously not like them.

But that Sunday in 1998, I was given a taste of an eternal truth. For a single and everlasting moment in time, I belonged. Not because I was born in Pinar del Río and was finally standing on Cuban soil but because of my Catholic faith. I belonged, I was one with "my" people, because of the Eucharist we shared, because the body of Christ, which we had just received, made us, truly, one body in Christ.

I was born on Fidel Castro's thirty-fourth birthday. In a very real sense, my life and my sense of self have been critically shaped by this stranger whose politics and public moral choices made me an immigrant at the age of two, a refugee, without a physical home. Like the Israelites in the Old Testament, I moved from place to place. As a contemporary nomad, I grew up while changing homes and moving from school to school—new towns, new states, even new countries. I never lived in a home for longer than three years. And I was enrolled as a student in whatever Catholic school employed my mother as a teacher, which meant I did a lot of two-year stints until I went to high school. As I look back on my early years, I realize that once my parents left their homeland in their mid-thirties, they could call no other place home. Yet I am also aware that this reality, which created a deep emotional and spiritual hunger in me for somewhere to call home, also blessed me with what I now call a pilgrim heart.

Somehow, I have always known that I'm here, in this life, yet on my way to somewhere else. Even as I strive to understand how to heal the pain caused by my longing for home, I remain thankful that my spirit, my heart of hearts, knows it will never feel at home in this life. In a very real way, all of life is a metaphor for the spiritual journey. My hunger for home, my need for security and intimacy and stability, is nothing less than God's way of sending me a personal call, an invitation, to seek him and to set my eyes on my eternal home.

The Tourist Transformed into Pilgrim

Whether you are a Christian seeking to grow in holiness or a non-Christian still struggling with the fundamental questions of meaning and existence, we would like to pose two questions as you journey through this book: Do you want to live as a tourist or a pilgrim? What does the journey mean for you?

Minnesota State University economist Gerald Smith has described some basic differences between life lived as a tourist and life lived as a pilgrim. The tourist's final goal is to fulfill as many desires as possible. Tourists seek entertainment and adventure as ends in themselves. The pilgrim, on the other hand, sees each journey as part of the greater quest toward the mysterious destination called home. Pilgrims desire true happiness, and that desire leads them into self-awareness and eventually to rest and fullness in communion with God.

Because the tourist and the pilgrim have fundamentally different goals, they will have different approaches to any journey. The tourist tries to figure out how to pack it all in; in other words, how to fulfill as many desires as possible given the constraints of the situation. For example, with three days in London and a thousand dollars to spend, what is the best way to allocate time and money to maximize the satisfaction of one's desires and preferences? Or with a medical degree, an annual income of a hundred thousand dollars, and a family, how does a person milk life for all it's worth? The pilgrim tries to discover the highest good and to figure out how to form habits conducive to achieving that good. The pilgrim may be a wealthy doctor who travels to London regularly to dine and attend the theater. There is nothing inherently wrong with such a trip. The pilgrim, however, knows that jetting off to Europe will never satisfy the deepest desires of the heart. Like St. Augustine, the pilgrim knows that the heart will remain restless until it rests in its highest good, which is God.

Another example of the pilgrim is found in the story of Jesus' birth. The Magi, who were open to the transcendent, left all their possessions behind and set out on a pilgrimage to an unknown destination in a strange land, a journey that culminated, inconceivably, at a manger in a Bethlehem stable.

We guess that most of you reading this book are like Michael and me: you desire the pilgrim life, even if in fits and starts. Some of you, whether consciously or subconsciously, may opt for the life of the tourist. And if you do not choose consciously, you will by default fall into the tourist life, especially in a consumerist society such as ours, which glorifies consumption, immediate gratification, wealth, and sex appeal. It is, however, possible to be tourists for most of our lives and to become pilgrims only at the end of life's journey. This is the story of the redemption, reflected so eloquently in the story of the prodigal son, which Michael talks about in chapter 4. It is also possible to be pilgrims most of our lives, only to abandon the quest and settle for the life of the tourist at

the end. This is the story of sin and the lack of persever-
ance, revealed most starkly in the fall of Jesus' disciple
Judas, who betrayed Jesus in the end.

We have known avowed atheists who, although still far
short of acknowledging God, were clearly pilgrims
searching for answers to life's fundamental questions. We
have also known Christians who, while not abandoning
the ritualistic exercise of the faith, have abandoned the
pilgrim life in favor of the more "comfortable" life of the
tourist.

Even intentional pilgrims—Michael and I place ourselves
in this category—spend much of our earthly lives as tourists.
In fact, a vital part of the journey is the gradual transformation from tourist into pilgrim. In the act of surrendering to
God, we open ourselves to his grace so that it might aid us in
greater understanding of the mysteries we profess and help
us conform our will to God's. Throughout our lives, we
bounce back and forth between tourist and pilgrim, between
the well-trodden path and the road less taken.

At the journey's beginning, we are more tourist than
pilgrim, still very much attached to (or even enslaved by)
the satisfaction of our temporal desires. Although these
desires manifest themselves in different ways in each of
us, they all stem from a deeply felt need for acceptance
and belonging, coupled with a sense of inadequacy. As
parents of four children between ages fourteen and
twenty, we see this tension lived out daily. A teenager
wants cars, ski trips, the latest clothes, boyfriends or girl-
friends, good grades (or, in some cases, bad grades), and
many other things. Even a hello from one of the cool
kids—especially when witnessed by others—can be a
highly sought-after prize. Michael and I have "ruined the
lives" of our teenagers on more than one occasion. At age

sixteen, more than one of our children wanted a car. We explained that we didn't need a third car because I worked from home, Michael worked only ten miles away, and if all else failed, as their dad continues to remind them, the school district provided a big yellow taxi to cart children to school and back home again. Nevertheless, the children persistently let us know that denying them a car ruins their lives because all their friends have cars and only nerds ride the bus or get rides from their parents.

This life as a tourist is not just a teenage phenomenon. It begins much earlier and continues well into adulthood. In twenty-first-century America, most of us know of someone who has abandoned spouse and children to find him- or herself. Many people become obsessed with owning the latest cars and elaborate houses, staying fit and youthful, and being able to go on luxury vacations. Others have a perpetual desire to fix the problems of friends and to feel inadequate when rebuffed. Still others desire constant attention from those around them and feel unloved if they don't receive it.

Michael describes his struggle this way:

> Like many, I struggle with a deep-seated desire for my work to be valued, and this can lead to petty jealousy and a lack of appreciation for the gifts I have been given. Typical questions that I might ask myself when I am cruising through life as a tourist include: Charlie was invited to speak at the conference—why wasn't I? Nick's work was praised in a recent article. Mine was better—why wasn't it even mentioned? Why was Ingrid given that position rather than me? In short, when I'm a tourist, my happiness depends on acquiring the goods and satisfying the preferences deemed important by my

local tourist bureau. My adequacy and belonging
depend on measuring up to standards imposed on
me by fallible human marketing agents and my
own heavy baggage. Deep down, I know that I can
never fully fit in, that I will never fully measure up
to someone else's external standard.

When we realize how unsatisfied we remain, even with all
our possessions, activities, and rewards, some of us just
work harder to get more of the same. Others give up, preferring to numb their pain with distractions, some more
dangerous than others.

The only real solution to these tourist tendencies,
however, is to develop a pilgrim heart. This requires, first
of all, that we understand ourselves.

The Longing That Leads Us

The New York Times Magazine described it as the "most
famous work of American art that almost nobody has ever
seen in the flesh" (Kimmelman, p. 40). In the shape of a
gigantic coil 1,500 feet long, the "famous work of art" is
made of 6,650 tons of black basalt and earth and is located
sixteen miles away from any sign of civilization. The spec-
tacular "earthwork" sculpture by Robert Smithson proj-
ects into the remote shallows of the Great Salt Lake in
Utah and is appropriately named *Spiral Jetty*.

Anticipating that the level of the water, which is the
color of rosé due to algae, would rise and fall, the artist
also envisioned that the residue of salt crystals would
cause the black rocks of his sculpture to glisten in white
whenever the water level dropped. What Smithson mis-
calculated, however, was the water level. After it was finished in 1970, *Spiral Jetty* remained visible for only two

years before it became submerged, which is how it has remained almost all the time over the past thirty years. Then, in 2002, the great drought in the West not only caused the Great Salt Lake to drop to its lowest level in many years, but also unearthed this example of an art movement that was befittingly dubbed "earth art." Artists like Smithson hoped to transform the landscape of the American West into an outdoor art gallery of sorts.

But as the *New York Times Magazine* article pointed out, *Spiral Jetty* and other earth art pieces are much more than unusual sculptures or tourist attractions. They are "implicitly spiritual" in that, existing far away from everything else, they require pilgrimages to the remote sites where they are usually located. "The trip to see them [becomes] integral to the art" (Kimmelman, p. 42).

Because of its size and design, the best view of *Spiral Jetty* is from the air. I can't imagine what this massive creation would look like in person, but in print, the photo that most impressed me was one taken from directly above the sculpture. The blend of red, white, and blue created in this amazing outdoor setting is splendid. Yet it is the shape of the art itself that captivates me. It reminds me of the inward spiral of a conch shell or the way water flows counterclockwise down the drain in the Southern Hemisphere. The shape of the object speaks to me of something deeper: movement to an inner center.

Each of us has a center, a hollow deep within. Like the inward movement that shapes Smithson's *Spiral Jetty*, our own journey inward has a certain shape. That shape is determined by specific facts: the place of our birth; our family of origin; our place in the family's birth order; our family's circumstances during our childhood; momentous or life-changing events or illnesses; and sometimes, unspeakable hurts that were inflicted upon us. And each of us has developed survival techniques in order to function within our very specific life and family circumstances.

Not only does our journey have a specific shape, but each life has a specific makeup. In the way we might study the makeup of *Spiral Jetty*—its materials and colors—we study our own makeup as well. There are many personality indicators, for example, that give new language and understanding to why I act the way I do. Although I have taken a lot of these tests over the years, the personality indicator that has offered me perhaps the most valuable perspective and insight has been the Enneagram. By becoming aware and acknowledging that I am a Type Four (sometimes called the tragic romantic or the artist), I have been able to name truths about myself that I have always known in my heart but for which I had no vocabulary.

All these personality typologies are meant to be tools for the spiritual journey. While no one test or procedure can provide a definitive label as to who I am, they all assist me in gaining specific and perhaps new language that may or may not lead me to a deeper awareness of myself. Most of us don't spend much time with self-analysis. In fact, if we err too much in one direction, it is in not giving the time and energy necessary to know ourselves and our God-given personalities, our needs, and our gifts.

Coming to know myself is, clearly, an important part of the spiritual journey. (And it is no coincidence that I often learn about who I truly am when I go on physical journeys. Travel itself is sometimes a great revealer—and shocker.) Yet as we grow in knowledge about ourselves, we also become more aware of that hollow, that space that holds not only our hurts but also our fears, our dreams, and our most fragile thoughts and feelings. At first, and then repeatedly at various times in life, we try to fill what we perceive as an empty hole, with people, or with acquiring things, or with excitement, or even with addictive behavior—all of which is temporarily satisfying.

Sometimes, in our desire to soothe the ache and fill the emptiness, we are content to give it a name, often in relation to a major event or personal crisis. For example, I have a deep hole inside me that aches because of my profound need for "home," born out of my experience as an immigrant. Or perhaps I have a yearning for intimate friendships because, as a child, I moved around a lot and was not able to maintain lasting friendships. Or perhaps my ache stems from being extremely sensitive to the needs and feelings of others around me—something I learned as the youngest child in a needy family.

But, ultimately, nothing can fill that longing. Nothing can make it feel better. And only the acknowledgment that it exists, that it is real—and that I cannot take care of it by myself—will help me move beyond despair, sadness, addiction, fear, and emptiness.

What I have come to understand is that not only is God already present in that hole inside of me, *God is the yearning itself*. Everything about my specific reality is part of God's divine and merciful plan to show me that he is already with me. *God is the path itself*. Just as something transforms an adventure into a pilgrimage and a tourist into a pilgrim, the awareness that God is the longing transforms my life quest from mere self-knowledge into a true pilgrimage. In the words of the German mystic Meister Eckhart: "No man desires anything so eagerly as God desires to bring men to the knowledge of himself. God is always ready, but we are very unready. God is near us, but we are far from him. God is within, and we are without. God is friendly—we are estranged. . . . Whoever seeks truth seeks God, whether he knows it or not."

For this reason, the first step in developing a pilgrim heart is self-knowledge. The pilgrim heart is focused on our inner journey home, to the God who is already with us. When we see life in this way, we can make the conscious decision to call the daily journey a pilgrimage, whether that journey is in the confines of a living room or across the ocean to a remote destination.

The Trust That Keeps Us Moving

As someone who has worked out of a home office for most of my adult life, I have developed an efficient routine for my workday. Before I ever come out of my bedroom in the morning, I take time for contemplative prayer. Sometimes I linger in my prayer space, reading. Depending on how early I begin my day, the routine may shift after that as I try to spend some morning time with my children before they head out to school. Perhaps I'll have a cup of coffee with my daughters as they eat breakfast, or manage a short conversation on the stairs with one of them while she waits for a ride to school.

Yet as soon as they leave the house, my routine once again becomes pretty set. I sit down to write in my journal, something called "morning pages," which I have adopted from Julia Cameron's book *The Artist's Way*. And immediately after journaling, I sit at my computer and allow myself to write no less than a whole page of whatever comes out. I don't open my e-mail. I don't play music. I don't use notes. I don't look at the stacks of work stuff around my desk. I consciously set it all aside in my mind, and I give myself the gift of opening my spirit to whatever words want to come out, whatever creation God has in mind for me that day.

As lovely as that concept may sound, in practice it is truly a tough personal discipline. Most of the time, I can handle with relative ease the discipline of ignoring the laundry or the dishes, separating housework from my work. I have had years of practice at that. But learning to sit at my desk and completely trust the art that God has placed inside me, allowing myself to be the conduit of God's creation—that is a discipline of the heart as well as of the mind or the will.

Trust is a discipline. I have to choose to trust. And I have to *learn* to choose to trust. I have to make a choice to open up my heart, often letting go of the familiar and the comfortable. I consciously choose to "take the plunge" and place myself and my well-being in the hands of someone else, be it my spouse, an intimate friend, or my God. This requires discipline in the sense that I have to work at making it a part of my regular mode of operation, a part of my daily living. I have to work at developing the attitude that fuels the actions I take throughout my day, like sitting at my desk waiting for whatever it is inside me that is ready to be spoken. My soul waits for God—and that involves trust.

Trust is also at the heart of what it means to live the way of a pilgrim.

This concept of living out trust about my craft and my art manifests itself both in how I operate and in my attitude toward work. Do I trust that I have a gift? Do I trust that God will show me how to use that gift, today and every day? Do I trust God enough to let go of my fears about what people may think of my work, what reviewers may say about my books? Letting go of doubts about myself and of the fears about my work is essential if I am going to allow God's creativity to work through my life.

And while fear never fully disappears, it is at those moments of letting go, of giving myself fully, in trust, to the heart of my writing, that this thing called inspiration happens. This sounds really esoteric, but inspiration is nothing more and nothing less than allowing God to act upon me and through me.

Handel wrote the *Messiah* in less than a month. Michelangelo sculpted *David* and the *Pietà* when he was merely in his twenties. When we hear these stories from history, we may admire these particular artists and even give them the label of "genius," but in doing so, we dismiss their example of surrender as relevant for our lives. These artists were spiritual men who opened their hearts, their spirits, and yes, their skills to the Great Creator. We, too, are called to do the same.

As specific as these concepts about the writing life may sound, the truths they embody are about living. Like a sculptor eagerly awaiting the beautiful image that wants to be birthed from the plain slab of stone, each of us has a one-of-a-kind spirit created by God that is waiting to burst forth. God created this unique spirit inside each of us for a reason. God needs us to live out who we are in the world. He needs me to be me, fully me, truly me—for my family, my neighbors, my workmates, my parish community, my city, my state. There are no coincidences. So everything about who I am—even my past, my experiences, my family—was given to me for a reason. And I have been placed within this reality for a reason, too.

Living with the heart of a pilgrim requires me to allow my spirit to be birthed into my world. And it demands that I trust the map that God has created for the pilgrimage called my life. This pilgrimage is not random or generic or communal, but personal and specific. I was birthed into this moment by a Creator whose vision for the world not only includes but requires me. I am an explicit part of his plan!

This brings me back to the discipline of trust. If I claim to be a follower of Jesus, a *disciple*, I must, by definition, learn to follow. This means I can and will practice the discipline of trusting in God's plan for my life. This means I choose to live out the discipline of trust in believing that every detail about who I am and about my day was given to me by a God who loves me and whose vision of the world needs me. St. Teresa Benedicta of the Cross (Edith Stein) said it this way: "Whatever did not fit in with my plan did lie within the plan of God. I have an ever deeper and firmer belief that nothing is merely an accident when seen in the light of God, that my whole life down to the smallest details has been marked out for me in the plan of Divine Providence and has a completely coherent meaning in God's all-seeing eyes. And so I am beginning to rejoice in the light of glory wherein this meaning will be unveiled to me" (Oben, p. 77).

I practice my trust every time I sit at my computer and ask God to send his Holy Spirit so that I may get out of the way and let God's words become mine. I live out this trust when I answer the phone or sit with my daughter or spend time with my aging parents. When I trust and open myself to God in each moment, I taste the meaning of true freedom. I have learned, also, that the more I practice this discipline of trust, the easier it is to see each situation, each person, with new eyes. I can't say that I fully "get it," but I will say that it gets easier as I open my hands, my eyes, my heart, a little more each day.

Trust not only helps me move through every "ordinary" day, it also keeps me moving on any other journeys I take. A physical pilgrimage through unfamiliar territory is an excellent lesson in trust—one reason that physical journeys can help us spiritually and that pilgrimage itself remains so relevant and popular. When I have traveled to other places, whether as a journalist or as a Catholic on a specific pilgrimage, I have had to accept whatever the road had to offer—the accommodations, the companions, the weather, and the tedious or dramatic situations. Being out of my normal environment teaches me trust in very concrete ways. If I choose to trust that God is watching over, even orchestrating, my journey, I can relax and enjoy the trip. I am also more open to the lessons of the spirit that God seeks to teach me. If I refuse to trust, however, the travel is tension filled and exhausting. Physical pilgrimage trains us in dramatic ways to trust the entire journey—both inward and outward—to God's care and plan.

The Load We Carry

Every once in a while during our Jubilee Year pilgrimage through Europe with our kids, I felt really old—too old to be backpacking my way from country to country with everything I "needed" literally on my back, including souvenirs! One particular day stands out in my memory. It was the day we arrived in the beautiful medieval city of Siena. In my limited Italian, I asked someone to give us directions to the convent where we had lodging reservations. From what I understood of the young woman's response, we could take a bus that would leave us near the place, and from there we could walk. So we took the bus, and it let us off somewhere in Siena.

As the streets became hillier and the backpack grew heavier, I stopped somebody else and asked once again for directions to the Alma Domus guesthouse at the Santuario di Santa Caterina. The older gentleman first smiled, no doubt at the unusual sight of a whole family of backpackers. Then, using his arms as much as his voice, he pointed and encouraged us in the direction that we were already walking. We continued for another long trek. But with every heavy step on the now steep terrain, I began to feel very old, much older than my then thirty-nine years of age. And I began to proclaim very demeaning things to myself in my head: *What were you thinking? People who backpack through Europe are young and childless, and they are in much better shape than you! You are never going to make it.* Finally, I stopped and asked one more person for directions to the convent. But this time, I couldn't grasp even one word of the response. Like the others before him, however, our Italian helper used his hands to point us in the same direction in which we were walking—except he added a twisting wave with his right hand at the end of the sentence. And I had no idea what that meant.

I now began to voice my demeaning and negative thoughts with my also-tired family, which was a very bad idea. In their attempts to encourage me, Michael and the children took turns seemingly dismissing and ignoring each of my concerns or comments, which only made me more frustrated—and tired, and old, and mean.

So I stopped walking and sat down on the ground, with my backpack still on my back. I did wait until we were away from traffic and in what looked like a small park on the side of the narrow road we had been walking.

Then I simply plopped down on the curb and declared to no one in particular, "I'm not moving from here until we know *exactly* how far we have to go—or until we agree to take a taxi to get there."

My dear Michael did what any civilized, caring husband would do. He looked at me, then walked away silently, going down the hill and off to the right, somewhere out of my sight. This left our tired and confused children straddled between two simple options: to pout with Mom or to walk with Dad.

And so they left me! Every one of them walked away, but not without first making some kind of (true) remark about my pouting. The sad thing is that I knew I was pouting, but I didn't care. I was too tired, and so I gave up. I wanted to walk, for once, without carrying what now felt like the weight of the world on my back. I wanted to know where we were, exactly, and where we were going. And more important, I wanted to be told how long it would take me to get there! Of course, I also wanted it all to happen instantly, immediately, and before it got dark.

After a few long minutes, Michael came back up the hill with a big smile on his face. Trying very hard not to sound condescending or mocking, he walked over, sat next to me, and said, "Honey, you will never believe how close we are."

It turned out that the distance from my little park to the entrance of the convent was, at most, a hundred feet. And since we were standing uphill from it, you could, literally, throw something from where we were, and have it land in the small courtyard at the entrance of the convent. When Michael looked at my baffled face, he finally let out a laugh and added, "You know, you're going to find this very funny someday, and none of us will ever let you forget it! You realize that, don't you?"

Although at the time, carrying what felt like bricks on my back up and down the steep hills of Siena, nothing seemed very funny, eventually, I did find lots of humor in our adventure. I also remember that day as a major break-through for me in that it gave me a new metaphor about pilgrimage.

When I took off my backpack that Tuesday afternoon in Siena, I did not discover any huge item that I could dis-card and suddenly lighten my load for the rest of our trip. I pretty much had the items that I needed in my backpack. But the "bricks" I identified and finally left behind in Siena were just as real and perhaps much harder to unload than an extra pair of shoes.

Clearly, if my perspective had been different—more open, less pessimistic, less focused on how old or tired I felt—our relatively short venture between the train sta-tion and the Santuario di Santa Caterina would have been a much more pleasant experience, for all of us. I allowed myself to get stuck in the groove of repetitive whining. And as the kids say, my attitude sucked. How often is this true in my daily life?

I often choose to see the day-to-day events of my life as bricks that make my load impossible to carry. Every-thing becomes a burden, like the backpack full of nega-tivity that I carried through the streets of Siena. Everyone becomes a nuisance. Every surprise is an interruption, and every phone call, someone's obvious desire to ruin my life and my day. Rather than trusting that surely God will grant me "my daily bread," what I need that day, I go through the day hungry and tired and feeling old in atti-tude and perspective.

So what do I have in my daily backpack?

While the objects I choose for my daily walk are important and significant, they are so because they reflect the things I hold dear. The objects in my life, from what house I live in to what things I think I can't do without, are only a reflection of the pack I carry on my inner, spiritual journey and how light or heavy it is.

I don't usually have a problem letting go of material things. While I enjoy a nice car or having nice things in our house—and I especially enjoy the ability to travel—I am happy whether I have these things or not. This is not one of my battles.

So maybe I am not as materialistic as some people. However, I carry another burden that is just as taxing. It is the question, Am I good enough? A little voice sings this out-of-tune melody in my ear: *I am not worthy (of a nice home, cars, things, trips). I am not good enough to be loved. I will never be good enough and don't deserve the goodness and bounty that God gives me every day.* This spiritual burden is one I wish I didn't carry in my backpack, but I do, all too often. It's a pattern, a habit really, that I have allowed for so long to shape my behavior that I have to consciously and deliberately fight it almost daily. Believing with my heart that what I am is enough, that God already loves me, is a true act of faith. Some days, God's grace is so real and so present to me that making this statement of faith is not very difficult. But more often than not, I step out in faith and plead that God will fill the hole that is my unbelief. Quite simply, proclaiming this statement—*What I am is already enough*—is a spiritual truth that shapes and affects my "backpack."

So when I ask myself what I carry in my daily backpack, I'm certainly examining the material aspects of that question. What things in my life do I hold dear? What are my earthly treasures? But I'm also looking for what spiritual and emotional objects I carry that make my load easier or heavier. In my daily luggage is there an attitude of negativity or of hope? What regrets from my childhood, or from last week, am I hanging on to? What prevents me from having an attitude of thanksgiving and an awareness of divine abundance in my life? What can I choose to let go of, right now, even if it makes its way back into my backpack later?

An English mystic of the fourteenth century, Juliana of Norwich said that the Lord answered all her questions and doubts by saying, "I may make all things well, and I can make all things well, and I shall make all things well, and I will make all things well, and you will see yourself that every kind of thing will be well" (*Showings*, p. 229). This statement reveals an attitude of trust in the final truth that God will make all things well in eternity. And it conveys trust that in this moment, all things are *already* well, even the things that I do not understand or that I find difficult to handle. God is walking with me. That is why all is well.

My responsibility is to examine my backpack daily. I wish I carried only the things that are truly important to me: my faith, my love for my family, a generous spirit, and a welcoming heart for God and for the people God gives me daily. But the truth is that sorting through and deciding what is really essential in my backpack is a daily chore that sometimes I do very well and other days I fail at miserably. As Paul notes in his letter to the church in Rome, "What happens is that I do, not the good I will to do, but the evil I do not intend. . . . [E]ven though I want to do what is right, a law that leads to wrongdoing is always ready at hand" (Rom 7:19–21, NAB, 1971 edition). Seems like I'm in good company!

But as Paul also reminds me, it is with the grace of the Spirit who dwells within me that I can allow God's love to be my pilgrim's guide on my daily backpacking through life. Being at peace with my life's journey is not something that will come when I have control over all the details and circumstances. Instead, it means that I acknowledge my lack of control—and I choose to trust in a God who will walk the way with me, no matter what happens. What I *can* choose is what goes into my backpack as I travel. I can allow useless things and circumstances to weigh me down: anger, frustration, people I have to forgive, regrets, hurts I can't let go of. Or I can choose to leave those heavy and cumbersome bricks behind and to pack only what is critical for my journey: faith, patience, daily prayer, reading my Bible, living out my responsibilities to my family.

When we left Siena three days later, I hesitated for a moment as we walked past the small park and up the hill, wondering if I really wasn't good enough to do our backpacking pilgrimage. Before the demon of fear could fly, however, I instinctively began to say out loud, one by one, things I was thankful for. With every step I took, I began to name everything for which I was thankful—beginning with being thankful for my breath, for being able to walk, for my ability to hold hands with Michael, for the clothes I had on, for the smells around me, for the breeze against my face, for the small flower in the sidewalk, for my comfortable tennis shoes. Nothing was too small or insignificant to become an object of thanksgiving!

The Irish band U2 has a perfect song for the backpack metaphor: "Walk On." In beautiful and poetic images, it describes my daily experience of examining my backpack, encouraging me to lighten the load and leave everything behind and suggesting that the only thing filling the backpack and weighing it down are those things I can't yet surrender.

The Present Moment, Which Frees Us

Perhaps no other word in our language is used and abused as much as the word *freedom*. We use it to demand our rights. We claim it as a defense against other people or another group's oppression. Freedom, the state of being free, independent, is synonymous with liberty. We define it as one of our natural and unalienable privileges. But freedom from what? Or perhaps more important, freedom *for* what?

As a Cuban American immigrant, I grew up hearing the word *freedom* often and used broadly in many of our family's discussions. From my earliest memories, my parents made sure that my brother and I heard over and over again the stories of how our family left Cuba, with emphasis on the *why*. Mom and Dad wanted to make sure we understood that they chose to face an unknown future in a new country with a new language because they believed it was important to seek freedom, to live in a country where they could practice their Catholic faith and share it openly with their children.

Yet as crucial and essential as political freedom is in allowing for personal rights, on its own, it does not ensure true personal freedom.

Because we are pilgrims and disciples of Jesus, the road to freedom hinges on our trust in God's personal and unconditional love. Trust is our instrument, our path. Love is the foundation.

The key to true freedom is learning to live fully and completely in the present moment. In the wonderful book *Legacy of the Heart: The Spiritual Advantages of a Painful*

Childhood, Wayne Muller calls this the "discipline of mindfulness," which is an extremely appropriate image. It takes a lot of discipline to live in *this* moment, neither worrying about the future nor allowing regret or hurt from the past to dictate my present. The discipline of mindfulness "invites us to cultivate a deep love and affection for paying attention to the daily, precious moments of our lives, allowing us to receive and experience each new moment in a fresh way. . . . When we touch all we feel and all we are with mindful, loving attention in the present moment, we are able to be set free from the demons of our remembered smallness, free to grow and change, and to blossom in ways we never dreamed possible" (pp. 146–47).

This is true freedom! Real freedom comes when we wake up to the present, when we become aware of this very instant, as it is, right now. We don't have to wait to understand all the psychological implications of our childhood before we can be healed, before we can open ourselves to the love that God has for us right now, right here. We don't have to wait to belong. We are already home, in this breath, in this moment. That's where God is. As Trappist monk and poet Thomas Merton once said, "[T]here are no levels. Any moment you can break through into the underlying unity which is God" (Muller, *Legacy of the Heart*, p. 94).

A pilgrim heart demands many things from my everyday journey. I must be willing to examine and lighten my load as I travel. God will show me what this means. I am invited to trust that God will give me what I need for the journey and to feed and strengthen my pilgrim heart with the sacramental "tools" available to me, particularly the Eucharist. Perhaps most important of all, I will choose to trust in God's presence in my every breath, daily, over and over again. God will bless my desire to surrender what is familiar and comfortable in return for whatever new surprises my Creator has in mind for me.

I choose to open myself to healing and love and hope, trusting that this will lead me to true freedom, even though I know this also opens my heart to feel hurt and pain and sorrow. I choose to trust in what will happen, in what could happen. But more important, I choose to trust in a God who wants to be present in whatever does happen. And when I do, I will be shown firsthand the great and marvelous things that God has in mind for those who love him.

Michael and I have developed the wonderful habit of going on walks by ourselves at the end of the day. At first, these walks offered us a time when we could talk without children or household interruptions, the kind of conversations that actually have a beginning *and* an end! Over time, however, our walks have become a way for Michael and me to touch base with each other. We check up on the activities of the day, yes. But we also check up on how we are *really* doing.

I especially love it when we walk at night. It's such a glorious time of day. Even in the hot Oklahoma summers, there remains a sense of freshness at nightfall. And in autumn, my favorite season, I rejoice as all my senses are awakened on our daily evening walks. I smell the home fires. I look up and watch the leaves raining down on us. I hear and feel the crunch of leaves blanketing the sidewalks. I feel the cool air tenderly brushing against my face. Few things can beat the peaceful feeling of walking through the neighborhood next to my husband in the dark of night and glancing periodically at a star-spangled firmament.

Some of the streets in our neighborhood where we regularly walk have few or no streetlights, amplifying to the highest degree the light–dark contrast that unfolds above and around us. This deep and complete darkness only enhances the effect of twinkling lights hanging perfectly, like Christmas ornaments, on a black and endless veil. We've all heard that a candle becomes, or at least seems, the most brilliant when set in a dark room. But it's more than that. It is *because* there is darkness that we find and recognize the light. In a very real sense, we learn to appreciate light because our own personal experience has shown us the depth of darkness. "You do not have to sit outside in the dark," writes novelist Annie Dillard. "If, however, you want to look at the stars, you will find that darkness is necessary" (Dillard, *Teaching a Stone to Talk*, p. 43). Meister Eckhart said it this way: "Truly it is in the darkness that one finds the light, so when we are in sorrow, then this light is nearest all to us" (Cameron, *Blessings*, p. 171).

This truth may seem like small immediate consolation when we are walking a path of sorrow and pain and when our daily load seems too heavy to bear. But the reality is that we are pilgrims in transit through a temporary home, and often the road itself may be unfamiliar. It is precisely at moments when we cannot even see the path in the dark void of our hurt and distress that the light is nearest to us. This is a truth we must trust, especially when we cannot see, and it is perhaps one of the most difficult things we will ever do.

In his many books, contemporary author Henri Nouwen often reminds us to live our wounds and, above all, to trust that the capacity of our heart will always be greater than our wounds. "The great challenge is living your wounds through instead of thinking them through. It is better to cry than to worry, better to feel your wounds deeply than to understand them, better to let them enter into your silence than to talk about them," he wrote in *The Inner Voice of Love*. "The choice you constantly face is whether you are taking your hurts to your head or to your heart. . . . You have to let go of the need to stay in control of your pain and trust in the healing power of your heart" (pp. 109–10)

The difference between whether we live our lives as pilgrims or simply as tourists lies in the journey of life inside us. Our challenges will remain the same. Our life situations, problems, catastrophes, successes, and joys will likely remain unchanged. No one promises that things will be perfect or that our pain will disappear. Yet whether we acknowledge God or not, God is present through it all, every day. In the light and shining moments of our life—as well as in the depth of our despair—God is there. This is the truth that we can cling to. This is our beacon in the darkness. Our decision to believe in this is the one act, the one decision, that changes us and transforms us from mere adventurers into pilgrims.

There is simply nothing easy about trust at all. It is a decision to leap not away from, but directly *into*, the darkness I fear most. Faith is the radical choice to stay with my pain because I trust in God's healing and loving promise to me. This trust requires nothing less than a mighty and blind leap of faith! And it is a jump into an unknown and unfamiliar territory that we make in full surrender, not once, but over and over throughout our lives. It is like driving on a bridge in deep and dense fog—we can't see what is ahead of us. We can't even tell how much longer the fog will last. We don't see the other side, though we believe it exists. We keep driving, steadily and carefully, trusting that the bridge will take us through the fog to the other side, crossing the deep water that surrounds us.

When we make a conscious decision to live in the present moment by embracing each day, each person we meet, each situation in front of us, we are, like Mary in her "Fiat," saying "yes" to the graces that God has for us today and every day. In the words of St. Ignatius, we step out with trust that "everything has the potential of calling forth in us a more loving response to our life forever with God" (Fleming, *Spiritual Exercises*, p. 27). It is this distinctive choice that makes us pilgrims in our everyday lives. Our spiritual pilgrimage is not a random meandering through the landscape of our life, but a deliberate inner journey calling us home to who we really are. As author Sue Monk Kidd notes in *When the Heart Waits*, "That's the sacred intent of life, of God—to move us continuously toward growth, toward recovering all that is lost and orphaned within us and restoring the divine image imprinted on our soul" (p. 4).

3

Knowing What
Pilgrimage to Make

~ María ~

Every once in a while, it becomes obvious to everyone at our home that I need to go walk a beach somewhere. It's hard to describe the yearning that calls to me from within my Caribbean island–girl bones. I long for the smell of the ocean, the feel of sand between my toes. I feel so tired, a type of weariness that can be renewed only by the breeze and by the gaze into eternity that sitting by the ocean offers me. This longing occurs every summer. And I've learned that as autumn unfolds into winter, I once again get this ailment that I've heard called, appropriately, "saltwater fever."

As I've explained to my husband and children, it's not a desire to run *away* from something—or someone—but an awareness of being invited to go *to* something. No matter what is going on in my life, good or bad, saltwater fever reminds me to breathe anew.

It's not so much that the ocean becomes a symbol for God or that being by the water is some kind of medicine for my spirit. It's much bigger than that. As I am drawn by my hunger to sit by the sea, I am reminded that it is irrelevant how full or empty I feel from the details of my life. This ritual reminds me that *I* cannot fill me, no matter how hard I try. Only God can. Only God ever will. When I yearn for the ocean with all my heart, I am called "home" to a truth much higher and much more essential than whether I feel "happy." Walking a beach and allowing the wonder of the ocean to awaken reverence and humility within me is a pilgrimage, in the most sacred sense.

Of course, a pilgrimage is not merely about the place; it's also about the journey itself. When I journey to the ocean, I practice being open and allowing transformation to happen. My very journey is a statement of faith, a public declaration of what is important to me.

At the same time, place is important. My regular longing leads me to a specific place: the seaside. And over the centuries, there have been a number of specific places that continuously invited believers and nonbelievers alike to come and touch the hand of God. A person doesn't pick the place. The place picks the person and invites her to come, be still, and know God in a new and unpredictable way. Many specific sites have extended an invitation throughout the centuries to literally hundreds of thousands of pilgrims, over and over again.

A turning point in the history of pilgrimages took place in the early 1800s when Marian apparitions flourished throughout Europe. Again and again, Mary appeared to people, and her message was simple: she asked Christians to repent and return to living the message of the gospel. It was not coincidental that many of the sites where Mary has reportedly appeared were places struggling for peace, such as Medjugorje, in Bosnia and

Herzegovina. Or, as in the appearance at Fátima, in Portugal, they have occurred at moments in world history when Christians needed an extra shot of hope, a reminder to focus on Jesus, in the midst of war and violence. Christians were invited to come and see. And they did. As the stories from these Marian sites became known, people began making pilgrimages to the actual sites where Mary appeared. In making those journeys, people responded to the spiritual yearning that is often difficult to describe.

Certain places become objects of pilgrimage because of miraculous events, or because they are associated with holy people, or because people who visit them are blessed with personal and profound miracles. Thus many nondescript places are transformed into worthy pilgrimage sites. And they continue to invite pilgrims during our present times. Come and see. Open yourself and become a pilgrim. Take your fears and your hopes and your prayers and expect blessed graces to happen. Through the centuries and across cultures, these holy sites and shrines have persistently asked pilgrims to open their spirits and their hearts to what God can do in their lives. Go ahead. Make the journey. Come and see—and expect to be spiritually transformed.

The Right Time—and the Right Motives

Is a traditional pilgrimage right for you? Should you travel to a specific religious or spiritual site on a special journey? How do you know when it's time to travel? And how do you know that you're being called to go on a pilgrimage?

My first answer is simple. Some things, you just know. There really is no other way to explain it. Something inside you simply yearns to go. You feel invited, even summoned, to make this particular journey to this particular place. You can't explain it to yourself, let alone to other people. Perhaps you've had this gut feeling for one week. Perhaps you've had it for one decade. If it is something major, like going to the Holy Land to follow the paths Jesus once walked, you are also aware that, in spite of all your fears, there's a sense of peace and wonder about the possibility.

Another way that you know you're being invited on a particular pilgrimage is that amazing "coincidences" begin to happen. You had never thought much about Fátima, Portugal, before. But suddenly it seems that the name is everywhere you turn. The travel section of your local paper does a special feature on Portugal, and it highlights people going on pilgrimage to Fátima. Your neighbor's aunt, who is visiting for a week, just came back from Fátima and can't stop talking about it. The mystery novel you're reading will have a weekend trip to Fátima. A television series about spies that you enjoy watching with your spouse presents the main character rescuing a friend in, you guessed it, Fátima.

There are no coincidences in life. When we have eyes to see, we will be amazed at the details that come together and the extent to which God will go in order to link our lives to his. When we look at all the events of our lives with open hearts and open eyes, we will see remarkable connections inviting us to experience new awareness of self and the world. Some people call it serendipity, the instance of making fortunate discoveries by accident. I call it the Holy Spirit acting in our lives. As Martin Luther King Jr. is reputed to have said, "All life is interrelated. All . . . are caught in an inescapable network of mutuality, tied in a single garment of destiny." If we could only see, God's hand would be suddenly visible and palpable everywhere, connecting us to our life with him and to one another.

I am *not* saying that every place featured in the travel section of the Sunday paper is beckoning us to go on pilgrimage! But I do believe that when all the accidental moments seem to connect and to bring to consciousness a common theme, you should pay attention to the stirrings of your heart. Listen to what God is saying to you in prayer. You will know. Really. God never wants to confuse us. We're the ones who complicate the data. And God will persist in his simple message of love to you, until your ears and your heart are ready to hear it.

Because my name is María de Lourdes (I was named after Our Lady of Lourdes), all my life I dreamed that one day I would visit the small town of Lourdes in France. When our family began to plan our itinerary and to name places we wanted to travel for our Jubilee Year, Lourdes was one of the top sites on my list. It didn't matter whether we did it at the beginning or at the end of our summer. What mattered to me was to go, to touch the grotto of Massabielle where Mary once stood and from where she spoke to fourteen-year-old Bernadette Soubirous. I desired with all my heart to celebrate Mass there, to thank God for the many ways that our Lady has been a part of my life throughout my life. I wanted to celebrate my name!

Mine was an unusual, or at least uncommon, reason to desire to make a pilgrimage to Lourdes. Most of the five million pilgrims who annually visit this out-of-the-way town on the edge of the Pyrenees do so seeking a physical healing. Since March 1, 1858, the church has recognized sixty-six miracles from the waters at Lourdes, and there have been another five thousand "inexplicable healings."

Faith. Doubt. Crisis. Turmoil. Sickness. Penance. Curiosity. Adventure. Thanksgiving. There are as many reasons for making a pilgrimage as there are pilgrims. Some people initially set out seeking a miracle cure for themselves, or perhaps travel to offer prayers and petitions on behalf of a loved one. Some journey to that distant destination to fulfill a promise. Others embark on the journey because they find themselves at a pivotal moment in their lives, and they hope for guidance, or an answer, or perhaps a renewed sense of self-discovery.

Are there any "bad" motives or reasons for wanting to make a pilgrimage? What kind of person "should" I be in order to make a pilgrimage? On the ancient road across northern Spain known as El Camino de Santiago, a document dating from the twelfth century boldly addresses these questions. Hanging on the wall of one *albergue*, or pilgrims' hostel, it declares its doors "open to all, well and ill, not only to Catholics, but to pagans, Jews, and heretics, the idler and the vagabond and, to put it shortly, the good and the wicked."

There can be a multitude of first motives that catapult you into this particular pilgrimage. The initial reasons are ultimately not as important as what happens to you as a pilgrim at the site—or on the journey. You have been invited. You have a desire to take this specific and personal journey to a certain destination. That's what matters.

Perhaps you find yourself questioning how noble your motives are for wanting to make this pilgrimage. Don't. I counter your question with another question. Are you letting your fears and your apprehensions about the unknown create convenient reasons or excuses for not making the pilgrimage?

Ultimately, if you are open to surprises, God will use your pilgrimage experience as an opportunity to bring you closer to him, regardless of your initial motives. Not even the greatest saint, no one—at least while he or she is alive on this Earth—has completely pure motives. As long as we go to God *as we are* and offer ourselves completely to him—our motives, our desires, our unnamed and even our subconscious reasons—everything will be used by God. Not even our "unworthy" motives can keep God from revealing his love to us. As Henri Nouwen points out in *The Return of the Prodigal Son:*

> The question is not "How am I to find God?" but "How am I to let myself be found by him?" The question is not "How am I to know God?" but "How am I to let myself be known by God?" And, finally, the question is not "How am I to love God?" but "How am I to let myself be loved by God?" God is looking into the distance for me, trying to find me, and longing to bring me home. . . . I am beginning to see how radically the character of my spiritual journey will change when I no longer think of God as hiding out and making it as difficult as possible for me to find him, but, instead, as the one who is looking for me while I am doing the hiding. (pp. 106–7)

If you think a traditional pilgrimage is right for you, you can approach it in several ways:

• Sign up for one of the many Catholic pilgrimages offered by tour companies (advantage: all the arrangements are made for you, including hotels, most meals, transportation, guides, Masses, and entry fees to the various places).

- Sign up for a Catholic pilgrimage tour sponsored by your parish or diocese (advantage: all of the above plus you get to experience the trip with your local community and a local priest).

- Organize a Catholic pilgrimage for your parish or diocese (advantage: you set the itinerary up front but leave most of the hassles at home, and you can control and maybe lower some of the costs).

- Strike out on your own and plan your pilgrimage without a packaged tour (advantage: you can set your own pace, get off the beaten path, and experience more of the local life).

A Shrine Closer to Home

You don't have to travel far to find a site worthy of pilgrimage. Such places are developing on their own all the time in a variety of situations. Here's the story of a site not far from my own home.

On the fourth anniversary of the bombing of the Alfred P. Murrah Federal Building, Oklahoma City archbishop Eusebius J. Beltran celebrated an anniversary Mass at the old cathedral, located directly across the street from the bombing site. The Mass was for the whole community, remembering in a special way the victims' families and the survivors of that shocking act of terrorism.

Even now, I feel strong emotions as I remember walking in by myself shortly before noon. Few people know that the original St. Joseph's church was actually located on the ground where the Murrah Building was constructed in 1977, the same piece of ground that also housed St. Joseph's

Catholic School—and even the bishop's office and the original St. Anthony Hospital, the first hospital in Indian Territory. I went to the anniversary Mass that day because I felt I had to, though I can't explain why. I certainly didn't have any obligation to do so. I don't think I'll ever be able to fully capture in words the feelings I still associate with the Murrah Building bombing.

I first went to the bombing site in downtown Oklahoma City the day of the bombing—April 19, 1995—to cover the news event as a correspondent for Catholic News Service, the national wire service for the Catholic press. I saw firsthand the destruction that turned this city in the Great Plains into a war zone—the armed soldiers; the bloody sidewalks; the smoking overturned cars; the grieving eyes of search-and-rescue team members as they walked out of the rubble that once was the Murrah Building. I smelled the evil in the air that night and felt sick to my stomach for days. I watched fellow journalists from around the globe four days later as they stepped out of their detached observer's role and held hands to sing "Amazing Grace" at the statewide prayer service attended by President Clinton.

A year after the bombing, it was certainly amazing grace that blessed me when the archbishop asked if I would be interested in writing a book related to the bombing. Commissioned by the archbishop, I began to collect stories from family, friends, and coworkers of three young victims of the bombing, all of whom had been active Catholics who had already, in their young lives, transformed their world and the lives of those who knew them. Working with the parents of these amazing young people—Mark Bolte, Valerie Koelsch, and Julie Welch— offered me many blessings, including the opportunity to experience true and honest hope in the midst of some of the worst evil I have ever seen. Through their willingness to open their lives and their hearts in the book, these parents not only shared with the rest of the world their journey of forgiveness and healing but also became for me living testimonials of redemption and resurrection. They taught me that there is, indeed, life after death—not only in everlasting life but also in the power of hope to bring life and light to the darkest moments of our journey on this Earth.

On April 19, 1999, four years after the bombing, I went again to downtown Oklahoma City. I had to go to St. Joseph's Old Cathedral to remember the lives that were lost, to remember the lives that were changed and transformed and scarred forever, and to remember the hope in the ashes and the light in the darkness of my own soul. I had to go and give thanks for those who had witnessed to me and transformed me through their lives and those who had transformed me through their deaths. Because of the faith of ordinary people who chose to live their lives in extraordinary ways, I was a different woman that Wednesday morning from the woman I had been on April 19, 1995.

After Mass, the congregation processed in silence across the street, where a fence divided the actual bombing site from what was once N.W. Fifth Street. Only the family members of those who had died and, on special occasions, select dignitaries were ever allowed inside the fence, on the actual bombing site. I hesitated by the fence, looking up and down at the remarkable sight of notes, posters, hats, T-shirts, pictures, ribbons, stuffed animals, and other mementos of victims' lives tied to the chainlink fence—holy items left by those who loved them and by those who never met them.

After a moment, I felt a hand on my arm and looked up to smile at Rosemary Koelsch, the mother of thirty-three-year-old Valerie Koelsch, one of the young people I came to know and love through work on my book. I was moved beyond words as Rosemary softly invited me to walk inside the fence with their family. I followed them, walking to the southeast corner of the grounds, roughly the area where Valerie's final moments would have been on the third floor of the Murrah Building. Valerie's office was located on the west side of the Federal Employees Credit Union, where she worked as marketing director, but a meeting that morning put her in the part of the building hardest hit by the bomb. Her parents, Rosemary and Harry, had attended St. Joseph's Catholic School on the site where the Murrah Building was later erected. "We've said that it's kind of holy ground down there," Harry once told me. "We went to school in that same spot that became our daughter's tomb."

There are few words to describe the awe of standing with the Koelsch family in silence at the site where their beloved Valerie and 167 other people had died, victims of a senseless act of hatred and evil. To this day, my eyes flood with tears as I remember that prayerful moment. I stood on holy ground, ground that was made sacred not only by the deaths of those 168 people but, above all, by the power of their lives. The faith of these faithful people converted darkness to light, despair to hope, death to life. As long as we remember the love for God of those who died—as long as we stand in silence and join our hearts to their prayers—we will continue to allow their faith and their spirits to live among us, to change us, to lead us to Christ, who is life eternal.

Although I have been down to the bombing site count-less times throughout the years, that was the only time I stood on that sacred ground. And it was at that moment that I realized I, too, had been walking a personal four-year pilgrimage. It was a journey of faith that took me from the sight of evil and the awareness of how one person's sin can change an entire community to a place of redemption and healing. My fellow pilgrims on the road were many: the victims and their stories, the survivors, the families of those who died, the countless volunteers and rescue workers whose lives were changed by their own experience of living with death. I can only pray, even now, that they may also experience the living grace that only hope in the eternal can bring.

The Oklahoma City bombing site is now a beautiful and impressive outdoor memorial, an official national site that is part of the National Park System. The memorial stands on a three-acre site that includes remnants of the original building. The field where the Murrah Building once stood is set between two large golden gates that stand like bookends, with the inscribed message: "We come here to remember those who were killed, those who survived and those changed forever. May all who leave here know the impact of violence. May this memorial offer comfort, strength, peace, hope, and serenity." The actual ground where the building stood is now a field of 168 empty glass and granite chairs, a poignant reminder of each life lost. The chairs are in nine rows, representing the nine floors of the building, and are set according to the floor on which those killed worked or were visiting. Next to the field of chairs, and still between the two gates, is a four-hundred-foot reflecting pool. The Survivor Tree, an American elm that withstood the blast, stands to the north of the site, a symbolic statement commemorating those who survived.

No person or government agency had to make an official pronouncement declaring the site of the Murrah Building bombing a local or national pilgrimage site. Just as at the site of the World Trade Center's twin towers in New York City, from the outset, visitors came to see with their own eyes the truth that television and newspaper reports could never fully convey. At the sight of the gutted building, they stood in spontaneous, somber silence, creating a soundless atmosphere that is simply not natural in the downtown of any city. No one had to be told to be quiet or to be careful or not to touch. The appropriateness of reverence, of veneration, was self-evident.

From around the state and around the world, they came, even years after the bombing and long before there was a refined national memorial. As beautiful and moving as the Oklahoma City National Memorial is, sometimes I think that it felt more appropriate to reflect and silently remember at the dusty and nondescript chainlink fence originally installed to protect the site, a piece of which is still standing. Named by locals simply "the Fence," this chainlink wall and makeshift memorial of flowers, crosses, pictures, and handwritten messages became a natural and spontaneous shrine, truly a pilgrimage site.

Perhaps they came as sightseers, at least on the surface. I am convinced, however, that what attracted people to the Fence and the bombing site was not the horror and evil that many of us saw there firsthand. Nor was it the historic event or what was at the time the worst act of terrorism on American soil. If that were the case, this place and this event would have remained simply an incident, no matter how huge or profound their impact.

Pilgrims seek an encounter with God, even if implicitly. I believe that people came—and still come—to the bombing site hoping to find God. They come seeking an answer to the question deep in their hearts: where was God on April 19, 1995? And if they choose an open heart, what they will find at the site is a living testimony of how the sacred prevailed over evil, how light and love were birthed from the ashes of despair. God was right there on April 19, 1995, suffering with those who hurt, searching for days with rescue workers in the rubble for a sign of life, ministering with local priests and chaplains to all who needed hope. God was the hands of the volunteer, the touch of the minister, and the eyes of the rescue worker. God's love was the glue that held hands together in prayer at the site. God is the hope that remains alive every time a victim's life and the gift they brought to their family and community are remembered. It is this truth that continues to transform gawkers and tourists to Oklahoma City into pilgrims.

Every city, town, and region has places that, like the Oklahoma City bombing site, show how God has acted in a way that is uniquely meaningful to its local people—the oldest church in the state, a Catholic monastery or religious community, a historic church dedicated to Mary, or perhaps the birthplace of a local holy man or woman.

A pilgrimage reminds us that we are loved, that we are not alone. Something about the place, the journey to it, the experience, reminds us that we are one in Christ, one body of faith, joined in our life's journey to many who came before us and to all who will follow us. A pilgrimage also reminds us, personally, that we belong to God and that we have a unique mission in life. There is a special reason for our existence. Because we make an act of faith to set out on the pilgrimage, when we go and see, we touch a piece of this truth—and we are transformed, renewed, and strengthened to continue in our everyday pilgrimage. A pilgrimage ultimately teaches us that the meaning of life is found not at the end of the journey but in the very journey itself.

This is why a pilgrimage destination or shrine does not necessarily have to be a church building, or even a declared religious site, as long as it calls us to conversion, challenging us to a new experience of God. A pilgrimage journey is simply a unique and symbolic physical effort in the great journey of human life toward God, and it must always guide the pilgrim to the heart of our faith, Jesus Christ, our Savior and source of all holiness. Sometimes pilgrims head out on a quest looking for specific results, perhaps healing or a miraculous experience of some kind. Often they travel to a place seeking something they cannot name—perhaps spiritual courage, an answer to a question, or a sacred vision. No matter how far or how close to home, when a pilgrimage involves traveling to a particular place, it is because the person has been invited to walk this particular journey, even when it's difficult to explain why.

A Shrine Built by a Faith Community

Because the concept of pilgrimage is prominent in all of the world's major religions—Christianity, Judaism, Islam, Hinduism, Buddhism—every country and region of the world has official sites of devotion, sacred places that are sought out and visited by pilgrims. In addition to those, there are nonofficial sites, such as the one in Oklahoma City, that nevertheless offer an encounter with the divine.

Yet sometimes a pilgrimage site is created not by history or by an event or because it is the hometown of someone in particular, but as a direct manifestation of the faith of a local community. In Unyang, South Korea, for example, there is a recently built sanctuary that was envisioned and established by the labor of a Catholic community, led by its parish pastor.

Korea does not have many or very well-known Marian sanctuaries, but the grotto of Unyang has already gained notoriety as a site dedicated to the Madonna. From the time that the parish was founded in 1927, the first pastor of the parish of Unyang envisioned making the nearby natural grotto in the mountains a place of devotion to Mary. Because of financial constraints, the project never moved forward. Then in 2001, the pastor Rev. Soe Jung-Woong and his parishioners literally picked up the shovel and began to work on the grotto, located adjacent to the parish of Unyang, in the Diocese of Pusan. When the pastor discovered that the deserted grotto was sometimes used as a place of worship by the local shamanists, he organized a group of parishioners and began cleaning out the dirt and overgrowth, emptying the grotto of rocks, and clearing the mud and weeds. The new grotto has retained its natural hillside beauty, though it now has an altar, seats made of tree trunks, and is decorated with Marian statues and images.

The visionary parishioners at Unyang also built a way of the cross that begins at the parish church and ends at the Marian grotto. Pilgrims who climb the steep incline and pray the way of the cross are rewarded by the message found in a fifteenth and final station: "You are special to me."

Unyang is a small and nondescript village in South Korea. It is not the site of any apparitions of our Lady, or known physical healings, or other special signs. Yet the grotto of Unyang has already become a well-known local pilgrimage site visited by many pilgrims. As one description of the Marian shrine notes, "[I]t is most appropriate to say that the Grotto of Unyang is a small miracle, for it was built with the sweat and faith of its parishioners."

A Shrine Honoring a Local Martyr

As we drove up to Okarche, Oklahoma, the first things I could see of the town were the grain elevators and the steeple cross tower of Holy Trinity Church. Located on the historic Chisholm Trail, Okarche takes its name from three Indian names: Oklahoma, Arapaho, and Cheyenne. Many of the town's original white settlers were German farmers hoping to make a life in this fertile piece of Indian Territory. Two months after the area was opened for settlement to the whites, about twenty Catholic families gathered for the first Mass in one of the farm homes in the Okarche area. This was the original Holy Trinity congregation, and a year later, a church structure was completed in the town.

But as beautiful as the current hundred-year-old Holy Trinity Church is, with its ornate high altar and impressive alabaster and bronze baptismal font, we were not there to admire the artistic value of this historic church. After pointing out the beauty of its architecture, our tour guide took our group of parishioners to the sanctuary to observe the bronze relief of Father Stanley Rother, Okarche's most famous and beloved son.

Martyred on July 28, 1981, at the Oklahoma mission in Santiago Atitlán, Guatemala, Stanley Rother will very likely one day become Oklahoma's first canonized saint. As part of the Jubilee Year celebrations, a group of parishioners from our home church, St. Thomas More University Parish in Norman, traveled to Okarche to visit Rother's parish and hometown and to pray at the simple grave in the parish cemetery where he is buried alongside other members of the Rother family.

Father Stanley Rother served the Catholic mission in Guatemala from June 1968 until his death. In a letter to the bishops of Tulsa and Oklahoma City dated September 1980, Father Rother commented on the political and antichurch climate in Guatemala:

> The reality is that we are in danger. But we don't know when or what form the government will use to further repress the Church. . . . Given the situation, I am not ready to leave here just yet. There is a chance that the Government will back off. If I get a direct threat or am told to leave, then I will go. But if it is my destiny that I should give my life here, then so be it. . . . I don't want to desert these people, and that is what will be said, even after all these years. There is still a lot of good that can be done under the circumstances. (Rother, p. 31)

And in his annual Christmas letter to the diocesan newspapers that same year, he concluded, "The shepherd cannot run at the first sign of danger. Pray for us that we may be a sign of the love of Christ for our people, that our presence among them will fortify them to endure these sufferings in preparation for the coming of the Kingdom" (Rother, p.55). Shortly after midnight on July 28, 1981, three tall men wearing masks entered the rectory at Santiago Atitlán and shot and killed Father Rother.

Although I have visited a fair number of cities and churches associated with the life of a saint, praying at the church where Father Rother was baptized, where he received his first communion and confirmation, just seemed different. Stanley Rother was a farm boy from an unremarkable town in western Oklahoma. He struggled as a student in his first year of studies at the seminary. He served the first five years of his priestly ministry without much notice in a series of obscure Oklahoma towns. Then everything changed when Father Rother answered the call to serve at the mission in Guatemala, finding his heart's vocation as missionary to the Tzutujil people.

Perhaps what made this visit different was seeing Father Rother's simple and ordinary origins. Perhaps it is the fact that you can still drive the one-hour road trip from Norman to Okarche and listen to Stanley Rother stories from those who knew him well, both family and friends. Ultimately, however, what made the experience a pilgrimage for me was the reminder that every person can, and ultimately does, make a difference in every person he meets.

Pilgrimage Sites in Your Own Backyard

During the Jubilee Year 2000, the Archdiocese of Oklahoma City designated ten specific places in the archdiocese as places of pilgrimage. Through an official "pilgrimage passport" designed by the archdiocese, Catholics were invited to read information on the significant practice of pilgrimage, learn about Pope John Paul II's Jubilee Year decree, examine an explanation on Jubilee indulgences and the sacrament of penance, and read prayers for pilgrims.

"We are reminded that the Church is a pilgrim Church and we are all pilgrims," stated the dedication to the "pilgrim passport" written by Archbishop Eusebius J. Beltran. "A pilgrim is one who makes a journey with religious motivation to a sacred site. As pilgrims of faith, we are guided and inspired by the Holy Spirit to follow the footsteps of Christ."

Because many people were not able to make a Jubilee Year pilgrimage to the holy places of Rome and Jerusalem, the Archdiocese of Oklahoma City designated ten closer-to-home alternative sites. These sites were chosen because of their historical significance, their beauty, or the role they currently play in our local church's worship.

Only 4.2 percent of Oklahoma's population is Catholic. So if the Archdiocese of Oklahoma City can list ten places worthy of being called pilgrimage destinations for Catholics in the western part of a relatively small state, we are confident that you, too, can find a pilgrimage site wherever you live. It is with this in mind that we list, at the end of appendix A, the ten places designated by the Archdiocese of Oklahoma City as pilgrimage destinations for the Jubilee Year. We hope this list will illustrate the variety of reasons that a location is defined as a pilgrimage destination. We also hope it will motivate you to research places in your own diocese!

Nonreligious Sites Worthy of Pilgrimage

It is a haunting yet stunning image: a lone Native American slumped forward on his horse, his warrior lance symbolically turned to the ground. *The End of the Trail* depicts a harrowing scene from our nation's history. The imposing image currently serves as the centerpiece of the National Cowboy & Western Heritage Museum in north Oklahoma City. As the museum's Web site explains, "The monumental 18' plaster sculpture was created for San Francisco's 1915 Panama-Pacific International Exposition and received the exposition's Gold Medal for sculpture."

To many people, the James Earle Fraser sculpture is a reverent memorial. Others view the image as a reminder of the subjugation that all Indian tribes suffered a century ago at the hands of whites.

There are many images like *The End of the Trail* in this exceptional museum that tell the story of the difficult relationship between Native Americans and the white settlers who conquered the vast lands of the American West. Yet perhaps no single event from that period is as shocking or as stirring as images portraying the displacement suffered by the southeastern tribes, forced by the federal Indian Removal Act of 1830 to relocate to Indian Territory (now the state of Oklahoma).

Although many tribes can tell similar stories, "Trail of Tears" refers specifically to the Cherokee tribe's ordeal: the Cherokee were forcibly removed from their land and obliged to trek hundreds of miles to resettle. According to a Trail of Tears Association Web site:

> In May 1838, federal troops and state militias began the roundup of the Cherokee into concentration camps. In spite of warnings to troops to treat the Cherokee kindly, the roundup proved harrowing. Families were separated—the elderly and ill forced out at gunpoint—people given only moments to collect cherished possessions. White looters followed, burning or occupying homesteads as Cherokees were led away. . . . No one knows how many died throughout the ordeal, but the trip was especially hard on infants, children and the elderly. Missionary doctor Elizur Butler, who accompanied the Cherokee, estimated that over 4,000 died—nearly a fifth of the Cherokee population. (www.rosecity.net/tears/trail/association/)

Almost 150 years later, the U.S. Congress declared this infamous route the Trail of Tears National Historic

Trail—an unusual yet undeniable pilgrimage path. When we allow ourselves to experience the underlying story found in historical sites such as this one, we not only learn the heart of the history but also encounter the suffering sustained by the people in this piece of our communal story. Walking the Trail of Tears invites us to experience this Cherokee story as a testimony to a people's courage. This type of experience also opens us, as people of faith, to see and encounter the hand of God present in moments of history that may normally stand outside our personal scope.

Like the Oklahoma City bombing memorial or the Trail of Tears National Historic Trail, local pilgrimage sites need not be designated as "official" pilgrimage sites or even labeled "religious" to be spiritually meaningful. They can take many different forms: a connection to a historical event, such as the place where Martin Luther King Jr. was shot; the home of a writer or the studio of a local artist; or even a museum, such as the United States Holocaust Memorial Museum in Washington, D.C. All of these places are pilgrimage sites because they not only touch something spiritual but also invite us to be transformed. They are means for us to experience compassion, purpose, beauty, pain, courage—by uniting ourselves to a person, an event, or a pivotal moment in history.

Local pilgrimages can also be intensely personal. Some of the most meaningful pilgrimages we have undertaken with our children involve our own family histories. Because I have moved so much in my life, it has been especially meaningful to take my children to the sites in Puerto Rico where I grew up: a home, a school, the church where I took my first communion, the cemetery where my grandparents are buried. Sharing these sites with my children has enabled me to share a piece of what I have called "home," a place where I personally encountered God.

While Michael's grandmother Hazel Ruth Lonis Scaperlanda was still alive, our family took many opportunities to travel with her and to listen to her stories. Great-Grandma took us to the San Jacinto monument where George Washington Lonis, a veteran of the Battle of San Jacinto, is named along with others fighting for Texas's independence. She showed us the home in Galveston, Texas, where she lived with her young family. She walked with us on the beach where once upon a time she roasted hot dogs with her kids for dinner during the summer months. And she told us her own childhood stories in her hometown, West Columbia. I remain extremely grateful that our four children not only had a great-grandmother for many years but also knew someone who celebrated life and faith with them through her own stories.

Whether the chosen destination be an "official" pilgrimage site, a "religious" or historical setting, or simply a place meaningful to you as an individual or to your family, what matters is your personal attitude and disposition. God's grace is, literally, everywhere. But it's up to us to open our eyes to the experience.

4

Learning from Pilgrims of the Bible

~ Michael ~

Each of us—in whatever town or city or during whatever period of history—is on a similar pilgrimage. Our circumstances are, of course, unique. We bring specific gifts and callings. Each of us carries specific luggage or "bricks" as well. Our particular cultural, political, and economic circumstances contribute to the uniqueness of our personal pilgrimage.

But the same questions press upon each heart. And it seems that certain journeys occur again and again, repeated from one generation to the next because the lessons they teach are universal and eternal. One place in which we find accounts of these pilgrimages is the Bible.

In this chapter, we will follow some of the most crucial pilgrimages in the Christian story, those of Adam and Eve, Abraham, Moses, Peter, Esther, Ruth, the prodigal son, and Mary. As we travel through these stories, our souls can comprehend what each pilgrim had to learn step by step. These journeys are ours not only because they are part of our history but also because the recounting of them can give us insight into the journeys we take even now.

We invite you to reread these accounts in their entirety from the Bible. We also invite you to enter into the mystery of the stories themselves so that you might

- give thanks to God for his relentless pursuit of stubborn humanity
- give thanks for the lives of all who have said yes to God's call throughout history, preparing the way for your own yes
- examine how you might have responded if you had been in the place of those in the story

Adam and Eve: The Journey out of Paradise (Genesis 1–3)

God invites each one of us, together with the whole human race, to be in relationship with him. We must journey toward that friendship because the relationship was severed by the sin of our first parents. Therefore, Adam and Eve's wayward wandering is the genesis for all other pilgrimages. For this reason, each of our own pilgrimages must be seen in the context of humanity's zigzagging journey back toward communion with God. We are not alone as prodigal sons and daughters who have lost our way.

After God created the human person in the divine image, he provided a home in the Garden of Eden and invited male and female "to cultivate and care for it" (Gn 2:15). As with everything else in the created order, there were boundaries beyond which danger lurked. Like any good parent, God informed Adam and Eve of the boundaries, forbidding them to eat the fruit of the tree of knowledge of good and evil. God also told them up front what would be the consequences of disobedience.

Respecting their freedom, God allowed Adam and Eve to reject his invitation, which they did by eating the forbidden fruit. As a result, they were exiled from the garden to toil and sweat and die. But even after their disobedience, it is clear that God watched over them, providing them with "leather garments [by] which he clothed them" and settling them in a new land (Gn 3:21).

These early chapters of the book of Genesis provide an unflattering account of why we are a pilgrim race. We, who were created in the divine image to be in relationship with God, have continually made choices that have corrupted our natures and severed that relationship. For us, the real pilgrimage is the return journey. These early chapters of the book of Genesis also give us great insight into the rhythm of the journey. God invites us, gives us total freedom to respond, watches over us whether we respond well or poorly, and continually calls us back when we make wrong choices.

Abraham: The Journey to Trust (Genesis 12–22)

Abram was seventy-five years old when God said to him, "Go forth from the land of your kinsfolk and from your father's house to a land that I will show you" (Gn 12:1). Sacred Scripture suggests that Abram was fairly well-to-do, with an unspecified amount of accumulated wealth and a household that included a number of slaves or servants. There is no evidence that Abram needed to leave his home for political or economic reasons. At a time when he was probably ready to relax and enjoy the fruits of his fortunes, his life was interrupted by a call to leave the familiar for the unknown.

This was the first moment of truth for Abram, and it is the first moment of truth for each and every pilgrim. For the downtrodden and weary with no place else to turn, God often comes as an oasis of comfort and rest. But for the comfortable, God often comes as an annoyance in the night: Francis of Assisi, leave your privileged nobility, embrace a life of poverty, and rebuild my church. Thomas More, leave your comfortable life at court as Henry VIII's right-hand man and hold fast to the faith, even if it means imprisonment and beheading. Mother Teresa, leave your middle-class teaching assignment and follow me into the gutters of Calcutta, where you will spend your life picking up lepers with your bare hands and taking them home to care for them.

God's invitation to Abram was, in essence, "Enter into a relationship with me, trust me, sojourn with me, and I will make of you a great nation, and I will bless you." If I had been Abram or Abram's attorney, I would have become suspicious right away. Is this a scam? Is this an attempt to lure an old man out into the desert, where it will be easier to dispossess him of his wealth? There is no indication in Scripture that the Lord and Abram had a prior relationship of trust and companionship, and there is no indication that Abram knew the Lord as the one true God who created heaven and earth. Why should he trust this offer? After all, children were the greatest blessing to these ancients, yet the elderly Abram and his wife had none. How could this god make a great nation out of

Abram if Abram had not even been blessed with progeny? Even if we had ironed out those details, I would have insisted that the Lord give me the exact itinerary. Then he and I would have gone down to the local AAA office to have them map out the best route, alerting us to all the possible construction delays. Their guidebooks would also tell us the best places to lay our heads each night of the journey. Having reached a concrete deal with God, I might have embarked on the journey.

How do I know that I would have reacted this way? Because I have reacted that way many times in the past. The most comical example I can give is from our Jubilee Year pilgrimage to Europe. Our children's passports needed to be renewed, and I was told that they would be back in plenty of time for the trip. I thought that *I* had this and every other aspect of our pilgrimage under control.

The illusion of control started slipping away in the few days before our departure. Rebekah's passport had not come in, but we couldn't get any information out of the passport office. With three days to go, we found out, through the help of a congressional staffer, that the passport office lacked the proper supporting documentation. I assumed that they misplaced Rebekah's old passport, which I had attached to the application. As I was rearranging our plans—Rebekah and I would fly to Houston, get her passport, and catch up with the rest of the family in Rome as soon as possible—it dawned on me that we were embarking on a *pilgrimage*. And for the first time in days, I laughed. A pilgrimage is about surrender, but I had fought hard to control nearly every aspect of the itinerary.

By a series of small miracles, everything worked out fine. Half an hour before Rebekah and I were to leave for Houston (about fifteen hours before the scheduled flight to

Europe), we got a call informing us that her passport had been issued earlier that day and would be sent to us by next-day delivery. The airport shuttle van and the Federal Express delivery van arrived at practically the same time the next morning, and we were on our way. A couple of days later, much to our surprise and joy, we were at the Pentecost Vigil Mass being celebrated by Pope John Paul II in St. Peter's Square. Our tenth-row seats came thanks to the good sisters at Casa Santa Brigida, where we were staying. Step by small step, I am still trying to learn from Abram's pilgrimage and to say yes to God, trusting that his itinerary is much better than anything I could have worked out on my own.

Fortunately for us, and for our salvation, Abram didn't have me for his lawyer, and he answered the call and "went as the LORD directed" (Gn 12:4), not knowing how the Lord would fulfill his promise, not knowing the destination, and not knowing what obstacles would impede the journey. Early in the journey, after famine had forced Abram out of his new home and into Egypt for a time, the Lord spoke to him and said, "I will make your descendants like the dust of the earth; if anyone could count the dust of the earth, your descendants too might be counted" (Gn 13:16). Still without a child, Abram continued the pilgrimage.

Years later, Abram finally mustered the courage to question God about the promise. "O Lord GOD," he asked, "what good will your gifts be, if I keep on being childless and have as my heir the steward of my house?" (Gn 15:2). The Lord replied, "No, . . . your own issue shall be your heir." God then said, "Look up at the sky and count the stars, if you can. Just so . . . shall your descendants be" (Gn 15:4–5). Despite the absurdity of this octogenarian becoming the patriarch of an unfathomably large family, Abram "put his faith in the LORD" (Gn 15:6).

Abram and Sarai, his wife, did waver in their faith. At one point, Sarai suggested that Abram father a child through the maid, Hagar, and Abram agreed. Like people so often do, they grew impatient, wanting to force the issue on their own terms. Ishmael was born of this union, and jealousy overtook Sarai, causing her to abuse Ishmael's mother, Hagar.

When Abram was ninety-nine years old, God approached him again, saying, "I am God the Almighty. Walk in my presence and be blameless. Between you and me I will establish my covenant, and I will multiply you exceedingly" (Gn 17:1–2). After Abram prostrated himself, God continued: "My covenant with you is this: you are to become the father of a host of nations. No longer shall you be called Abram; your name shall be Abraham, for I am making you the father of a host of nations" (Gn 17:4–5). God changed Sarai's name to Sarah and told Abraham that she would give birth to his child.

Had I been the pilgrim in this story, I would have been tempted to pick myself off the ground and remind God in a not-so-soft tone that he had been making this promise for twenty-four years. I'd demand to know where the goods were and when they would be delivered. "Yeah, yeah, dust, stars, father of nations! I was already old when you lured me out of my home, and now I'm nearly one hundred years old, and you are making the same old promise. Famine, exile, and a jealous wife are all I've gotten for my troubles." At the other end of the spectrum might be a person who would submit, but grudgingly, viewing God as a bully, giving in to him like a child whose lunch money is stolen day after day on the school playground.

Abraham, in contrast, remained prostrate and laughed, saying to himself, "Can a child be born to a man who is a hundred years old? Or can Sarah give birth at ninety?"

(Gn 17:17). He and God had developed a relationship; he trusted God and did what God asked, no matter how bizarre it must have seemed. We see a more vivid picture of the give-and-take in this relationship in their conversation over the impending destruction of Sodom and Gomorrah. Abraham pressed the Lord, asking if he would destroy the innocent along with the guilty. Abraham first asked if the Lord would spare the towns for the sake of fifty innocent people. After the Lord said yes, Abraham got a little bolder, saying, "See how I am presuming to speak to my Lord, though I am but dust and ashes!" (Gn 18:27). Abraham continued until the Lord agreed not to destroy Sodom and Gomorrah for the sake of ten innocent people.

The ultimate test in this long friendship still lay before them. God had promised to make Abraham's progeny as numerous as the stars in the sky, but now he was asking Abraham to sacrifice it all by offering his beloved son, Isaac, as a holocaust to God. How would you respond to such a request? What emotions would embroil you? God, in his own way and time, had fulfilled all his promises to Abraham, but now he seemed on the verge of taking it all away. I'm sure an anguished Abraham probably thought, at least for a fleeting moment, that none of this had been worth it. He probably wished that God had not called him to live as a foreigner in a strange land, promising things that now would never be fulfilled. If such thoughts crossed Abraham's mind, they did not dictate his action because he set out the next day to carry out the Lord's command.

For three agonizing days, Abraham and Isaac journeyed together to the place where Isaac was to be sacrificed. John of the Cross writes about the dark night of the soul. I cannot imagine it getting much darker—spending three days and probably sleepless nights, wanting to get there quickly to see how it would end but wanting to linger to spend more time with Isaac. The heartache, the anger, and the sense of betrayal must have been unbearable, and still Abraham journeyed on. This was his pilgrimage. He had journeyed this far with the Lord, and he wasn't going to turn back.

Isaac was old enough to ask, "Here are the fire and the wood, but where is the sheep for the holocaust?" Abraham answered, "God himself will provide the sheep for the holocaust" (Gn 22:7–8). Given the relationship that had developed between Abraham and God, I am sure that Abraham hoped and expected that God would provide a sheep to offer in place of Isaac. But he also would have feared that Isaac *was* the sheep to be slaughtered. God answered Abraham's anguished prayer and spared Isaac that day. The Lord also graced Abraham with a ram to be used as a substitute offering. And, through Abraham, Isaac, and their descendants, all the nations of the earth have found blessing, as God had promised.

I can imagine God saying to Abraham, "Your child is my gift to you, your life is my gift to you, and your vocation is my gift to you. If you try to possess them, they will end up possessing you. Love your child but entrust him completely to me. Cherish your vocation but let me lead your every step in fulfilling it. Because of my infinite love for you, trust me in the use of these gifts. Trust me, and I will lead you to a home so glorious that it is beyond all imagination."

God speaks to us in the same way. He reminds each of us that to live, we must surrender our whole life, including *all* our hopes, dreams, and aspirations, to the "architect and maker" (Heb 11:10) of our life. We must be free of all attachments so that we can freely embrace God and be embraced by God. As we reflect on Abraham's pilgrimage, we might ask ourselves what possesses us. What keeps us from responding with an unqualified yes to God's invitation? Over what part of our lives do we want to maintain control (or, more accurately, the illusion of control)? What holds us back from falling into the embrace of God's love? Certainly, raw hatred and jealousy can bind us. Often, however, the things that control us are much more subtle. Abraham's pilgrimage, for example, instructs us that having too tight a grip even on good things—our children, God's promises, or our God-given vocation—can bind us. After receiving great gifts from God, we then begin to fear that we will lose what we have gained, either through forces outside our control or as a result of our own inadequacies. In short, we do not trust God with the gifts he has given us. Our pilgrimage, like Abraham's, requires the step-by-step growth of our trust in the one who calls us to the journey.

Moses: The Journey to the Promised Land (Exodus 2–20)

Humanity's pilgrimage started with an invitation to one man. Abraham's response—his unqualified trust—allowed God's friendship to be extended to a whole nation. The relationship between God and Israel is a long and storied one, marked by this repeating pattern: God's invitation along with the gift of freedom; Israel's rejection of the invitation in a misuse of freedom (often accompanied by exile); God's watchfulness over his wayward people; and a renewal of the invitation, often through the voice of prophets. Any part of this history can serve as a meditation on pilgrimage, but as the Pontifical Council for the Pastoral Care of Migrants and Itinerant People said in its 1998 document *The Pilgrimage in the Great Jubilee*, the Exodic pilgrimage from slavery in Egypt to the Promised Land provides "the exemplary model of the history of salvation itself" (p. 6). Again, we ask you to engage the mystery of this pilgrimage, feeling the rhythms of God's call and Israel's response, making this part of your own pilgrim journey.

To set the stage, recall that toward the end of the book of Genesis, the Israelites journeyed to Egypt, where they lived peacefully. In the opening of the book of Exodus, a new pharaoh came to power in Egypt and, because he feared losing power to the foreigners, enslaved the prosperous Israelites. When the time came for God to invite the Israelites to leave their life of bondage and journey to freedom, God approached one man, calling him to lead them. We get some sense of Moses' character early in the story. The fact that he killed an Egyptian who had beaten an Israelite suggests both a temper and a thirst for justice. The fact that he fled to the desert to avoid punishment suggests either prudence or cowardice. In all pilgrimage stories, there is a sense that the pilgrim is an alien. With Moses, this was doubly so because he was a foreigner in Egypt, and after running away, he became a foreigner in Midian.

The call of Moses was marked by a dialogue between Moses and God, who revealed himself in the burning bush. The Lord said, "Come now! I will send you to Pharaoh to lead my people, the Israelites, out of Egypt" (Ex 3:10). Like so many of us, Moses did not receive his vocation well. "Who am I," he objected, "that I should go to Pharaoh and lead the Israelites out of Egypt?" (Ex 3:11). God's answer was not "I have chosen you because of your strength, wisdom, and courage." Instead, God simply replied, "I will be with you" (Ex 3:12). Moses persisted, objecting on two grounds: First, neither the Israelites nor the Egyptians would probably believe him; second, he was not the right guy for the job because, he said, "I have never been eloquent, neither in the past, nor recently, nor now . . . but I am slow of speech and tongue" (Ex 4:10). In answer to the first objection, God offered to display miraculous signs to the Israelites and Egyptians to confirm Moses' call. In answer to the second objection, God reminded Moses that it was he, the Lord, who gave the human person the ability of speech, commanding, "Go, then! It is I who will assist you in speaking and will teach you what you are to say" (Ex 4:12). Testing the Lord's patience, Moses persisted: "If you please, Lord, send someone else!" (Ex 4:13). Although now angry, the Lord did agree to appoint Moses' brother, Aaron, as spokesman. During this conversation, Moses also asked God his name. God replied, "I am who am" (Ex 3:14).

This exchange reveals a high degree of intimacy between God and Moses. Moses apparently was not afraid to engage his much stronger companion in the give-and-take of a frank discussion, bordering on argument. I see this in my own relationship with my children. By authority of my position (coupled, I suppose, with the relative size differential), I have power over my children. As long as they respect me and my parental position, I want them to be able to speak freely, even if it is to disagree or challenge me. The Father appears to desire the same type of relationship with his children. In an act of extreme intimacy, God revealed to Moses his essence: "I am who am."

Pilgrimage is not an easy road. External foes present many challenges and obstacles along the way, and an internal voice constantly raises doubts, making the pilgrim question the wisdom of leaving the known for the unknown. Through nine plagues—blood, frogs, gnats, flies, pestilence, boils, hail, locusts, and darkness—Pharaoh stood firm, refusing to let the Israelites leave. After the tenth plague, the death of the firstborn, Pharaoh finally relented and allowed the Israelites to leave. He later changed his mind and pursued the Israelites, to his destruction (Ex 14:5–28).

For these Israelites, internal doubts arose early. Even before the plagues visited the land, the Israelites were registering their first complaints against Moses and Aaron for stirring up trouble, saying, "You have brought us into bad odor with Pharaoh and his servants and have put a sword in their hands to slay us" (Ex 5:21). Later, with the Egyptians in hot pursuit, the Israelites grumbled, "Why did you bring us out of Egypt? Did we not tell you this in Egypt, when we said, 'Leave us alone. Let us serve the Egyptians'? Far better for us to be the slaves of the Egyptians than to die in the desert" (Ex 14:11–12). Despite God's many blessings in their lives, the Israelites "grumbled" again at the slightest inconvenience or hardship (Ex 15:24).

Abraham's bondage had been very subtle; his attachments hard to detect. The Israelites, in contrast, clearly displayed the nature of the pilgrim's problem. They had witnessed God's miraculous handiwork through ten plagues in which havoc had been wreaked on the Egyptians while the Israelites had been spared as promised. But fear overcame them at the first sighting of Pharaoh's chariots. Instead of trusting that God would deal with Pharaoh again as he had ten times before, they gave up hope, preferring the familiar, even if it was a life of slavery. Trust, or lack thereof, is again the key element.

Throughout the Exodus, God was with his people. He invited them out of slavery "into a good and spacious land, a land flowing with milk and honey" (Ex 3:8). At times, this pilgrim people praised God for his glorious protection, singing hymns of thanksgiving. But at the first sign of discomfort, they fell into despair again, renewing their complaint against Moses and Aaron: "Would that we had died at the LORD's hand in the land of Egypt, as we sat by our fleshpots and ate our fill of bread! But you had to lead us into this desert to make the whole community die of famine!" (Ex 16:3). They grumbled about the lack of food; God provided them with quail and manna. They then complained about the lack of water; God responded by supplying them with more than enough to quench their thirst.

This pattern repeated itself in the lives of the Israelites just as it does in our own lives. After the Israelites arrived at Mount Sinai, Moses reminded them of all the great things the Lord had done for them, and they responded, "Everything the LORD has said, we will do" (Ex 19:8). They repeated this pledge twice more after Moses received the Law from God (Ex 24:3, 7).

But when Moses went up on the mountain to receive the tablets, the people quickly forgot Moses and God. "When the people became aware of Moses' delay in coming down from the mountain, they gathered around Aaron and said to him, 'Come, make us a god who will be our leader; as for the man Moses who brought us out of the land of Egypt, we do not know what has happened to him'" (Ex 32:1). Aaron created a golden calf, and the people cried out, "This is your God, O Israel, who brought you out of the land of Egypt" (Ex 32:4).

The truth had been displayed repeatedly in marvelous ways before their eyes, yet this "stiff-necked" people, as God referred to them, preferred the illusion of God to the real thing; a golden calf to the God of the universe; slavery to freedom.

This reminds me of a scene in the movie *The Matrix*. The traitor knows the truth about the matrix. He knows that it is a computer-generated illusion meant to enslave humanity in an unconscious dream state so that their bodies can be used by the enemy to generate energy. Millions of people are living this lie inside the matrix. Those few outside the matrix live a meager existence as freedom fighters, attempting to liberate the human race from its bondage within the matrix. The traitor, who is living in freedom outside the matrix, is willing to trade that freedom for life in the matrix, where he can have the illusory sensation of eating a tender, juicy steak.

Attachment, desire, and lack of trust impede our journey toward full communion with God. For some of us it takes the form of an excessive attachment to one of God's gifts: a spouse, a child, a job, or material things. I would guess this was Abraham's temptation and the reason the Lord put him to the test. For others, it takes the form of a craving for perverse things: power, recreational sex, drugs, or violence. Worshipping a golden calf falls into that category. Why were the Israelites so ready to discard God in favor of the illusion of God? Why did the traitor yearn for the illusory comfort of the matrix? Why do we prefer slavery to the "land of milk and honey"? Why do we prefer our own gods to the God of the universe?

The pilgrim journey is marked by infidelity, yet God remains steadfast in his desire for communion with us.

Peter: The Journey to Strength and Maturity

Peter is one of my favorite saints. Through him, we see clearly how God has chosen and can use extremely fallible human beings for what would be impossible tasks without God's grace and protection.

Matthew and Mark give us a startling account of Jesus' call to discipleship, "Come after me, and I will make you fishers of men" (Mt 4:19; Mk 1:17), and of Peter's response, "At once they left their nets and followed him" (Mt 4:20). Luke and John fill in some of the details, suggesting that Jesus and Peter had already developed a relationship at the time Peter was called (compare Mt 4:18–20; Mk 1:16–18; Lk 4:38–39, 5:1–11; and Jn 1:35–42). From this, we see that Peter was open to a life of pilgrimage— to radically changing his life in response to God's call— but he wasn't quite as impulsive as we might think from reading only Matthew and Mark.

And it is clear throughout Peter's life that he needed God's grace if he (and the church) was to advance in faith. When Peter objected to Christ's impending suffering and death, Jesus rebuked him: "Get behind me, Satan! You are an obstacle to me. You are thinking not as God does, but as human beings do" (Mt 16:23). Notice that only four verses separate Peter as the rock and Peter as Satan's dupe. Peter the coward denied Christ three times rather than face a hostile crowd; he was scolded by Paul for not having the courage to eat with the Gentiles; and legend has it that he was trying to escape Rome during the persecution when Christ met him on the road and gave him the strength to return to his flock.

Peter also clearly responded to God's grace with a holy desire to follow Christ throughout his life, ending the journey as a martyr hanging upside down on a cross in Rome. When he fell, he followed Christ's example and picked up his cross and carried on. After denying Christ, he wept "bitterly" (Lk 22:62). When Peter heard of Christ's resurrection, he "ran to the tomb" (Lk 24:12). When Peter heard that the risen Lord awaited them on the Sea of Galilee, he "tucked in his garment, . . . and jumped into the sea," and swam to Jesus (Jn 21:7). And on Pentecost, Peter, filled with the Holy Spirit, courageously began the church's work of spreading the gospel to all nations (Acts 2:14–36).

As Peter's life illustrated, strength and maturity on the pilgrim walk require an openness to God's plan for our lives, humility to repent, and courage to pick ourselves up when we fail.

Esther: The Journey to Destiny

More than once, the Israelites were exiled. And more than once, Israel was on the brink of destruction, only to be saved by God's power and providence. Through the intercession of a woman named Esther, God's people were spared during one such period.

Esther was King Ahasuerus's queen. Following her cousin Mordecai's advice, she had not revealed her Jewish heritage or her relationship to Mordecai, to the king, or to anyone else in the royal household. Mordecai, who had been in favor with the king because of some help he had given him, got in trouble for not paying homage to the king's right-hand man, Haman. In anger, Haman had the king issue an order to have all the Jews in the vast empire killed in a single day.

In sackcloth and ashes, Mordecai petitioned Esther to intercede with King Ahasuerus on Israel's behalf. At first, she refused to intercede because anyone, including the queen, who entered the king's inner court without summons would be put to death "unless the king extend[ed] to him the golden scepter, thus sparing his life" (Est 4:11). Mordecai then told her that she would die unless she helped, but he also reminded her that "royal dignity" may have been bestowed on her for just this occasion (Est 4:14).

Esther agreed to see the king, even if it meant her death. But before she petitioned the king, she, Mordecai, and all the Jews prepared themselves with fasting and prayer. God did intervene in the king's heart, and Esther and the Israelites were spared.

Esther's story teaches us that we walk either with God or against God, we fast and pray, and we humbly submit our lives and our journey to the one who created us and gives us life.

Ruth: The Journey to Faithfulness

The book of Ruth provides a short but powerful meditation on pilgrimage and loving companionship. The story begins with Elimelech, his wife, Naomi, and their two sons migrating from Bethlehem to Moab because of famine. Elimelech dies, and the two sons marry Moabite women, Orpah and Ruth. Childless, the two sons die about ten years later. Naomi is left with nothing—no income and no heir to carry on the family name.

As Naomi is leaving Moab to return to Bethlehem, she says to her daughters-in-law, "Go back, each of you, to your mother's house! May the LORD be kind to you as you were to the departed and to me! May the LORD grant each of you a husband and a home in which you will find rest" (Ru 1:8–9). Naomi acts out of love for her daughters-in-law, knowing that for all intents and purposes, her life is over. "No, my daughters! my lot is too bitter for you" (Ru 1:13). After much sobbing, Orpah leaves, which in many respects is the rational thing to do.

Ruth stays. Upon her mother-in-law's insistence that she leave, Ruth says, "Do not ask me to abandon or forsake you! for wherever you go I will go, wherever you lodge I will lodge, your people shall be my people, and your God my God. Wherever you die I will die, and there be buried" (Ru 1:16–17). Ruth sacrifices everything for the love of her mother-in-law. In many ways, Naomi is as good as dead already, but Ruth remains her faithful companion. As it turns out, Ruth's fidelity to her mother-in-law in a seemingly impossible situation is instrumental in the unfolding of salvation history. Back in Bethlehem, Ruth marries Boaz and gives birth to Obed, who becomes the father of Jesse, who in turn becomes the father of King David.

Like Ruth, we are called to be faithful to those companions God has given us.

The Prodigal Son: The Journey to Forgiveness and Freedom

Henri Nouwen's *The Return of the Prodigal Son* is a wonderful book that explores this parable from three different angles at three different points in the author's life. Here we explore it from the vantage point of the prodigal and his crooked journey (Lk 15:11–32).

Like Adam and Eve's, the prodigal's pilgrimage took him off the farm. Rejecting his father, he asked for his inheritance (which one typically gets only after the death of the parent). Respecting the child's freedom, the father gave his son half of everything, and the son promptly squandered it on wine, women, and song. Starving, the son was desperate. "Coming to his senses" (Lk 15:17), the prodigal decided to return home, where he knew his father fed all the servants and treated them fairly.

The drama intensified when the pilgrimage took a 180-degree turn. The prodigal, in a posture we can learn from, knew that he was unworthy, and he decided to return home in repentance: "Father, I have sinned against heaven and against you. I no longer deserve to be called your son; treat me as you would treat one of your hired workers" (Lk 15:18–19). The father, who must have been watching longingly, saw the son when the son was still far off "and was filled with compassion. He *ran* to his son, embraced him and kissed him" (Lk 15:20, emphasis added). Then, addressing his servants, the father said, "Quickly bring the finest robe and put it on him; put a ring on his finger and sandals on his feet. Take the fattened calf and slaughter it. Then let us celebrate with a feast, because this son of mine was dead, and has come to life again" (Lk 15:22–24).

This one parable sums up the whole pilgrim journey. We, individually and as a society, misconstrue freedom as *freedom from* the rules of our father's house. Out of respect for us, our father allows us to leave, giving us everything we need for the journey. When we begin to realize that we have misused our freedom, we want to return home. We approach home with a heart full of gratitude for all that the father has done for us, and we also know that we are unworthy. The father greets us with anticipation and open arms. Through his love and forgiveness, we begin to learn that true freedom is *freedom to* live our lives in love.

Mary: The Journey to Ultimate Submission and Grace

Humanity's pilgrimage home started with God extending an invitation to Abraham. Abraham's response—his unqualified yes—allowed God's friendship to spread to a whole nation. The Israelites' pilgrimage prepared the way for Christ, and through Christ and his church, this friendship has spread to the entire human race. As María wrote in her book *The Seeker's Guide to Mary*, "God's promise to the aged and childless Abraham that his descendants would be more numerous than the stars in the sky was fulfilled through the birth of the Christ child, who came to reconcile all of the world with God" (p. 5).

As the history of the Jewish people unfolded toward what we now know as the first century and as the people anxiously awaited the Messiah, the drama intensified. One can sense the growing anticipation at the possibility of a new level of intimacy between God and the Israelites. Of course, their expectation of a messiah to free them from Roman oppression fell utterly short of the magnificence of God's unimaginable plan.

As with previous encounters with the human race, God issued his invitation through one person. Addressing Mary, the angel Gabriel said, "Hail, full of grace, the Lord is with thee: blessed art thou among women" (Lk 1:28 DV). After telling Mary not to fear, he continued: "Behold, you will conceive in your womb and bear a son, and you shall name him Jesus. He will be great and will be called Son of the Most High, and the Lord God will give him the throne of David his father, and he will rule over the house of Jacob forever, and of his kingdom there will be no end" (Lk 1:31–33). When Mary objected on the basis of her virginity, the angel assured her of God's assistance: "The holy Spirit will come upon you, and the power of the Most High will overshadow you" (Lk 1:35).

Raising the level of intimacy exponentially, the angel invited Mary—and through her, all Christians—to take God to the interior of her very being and there give birth to him for the world. "[T]he child to be born," the angel told Mary, "will be called holy, the Son of God" (Lk 1:35).

We get a taste of this intimacy in its eucharistic form in John's Gospel (6:56): "Whoever eats my flesh and drinks my blood remains in me and I in him." Looking back on it, we see that the bread and wine offered in sacrifice by Melchizedek, the Passover feast, and the manna in the desert all foreshadowed this level of intimacy, which God desires for the pilgrim.

Mary is the ideal pilgrim. Her profound yes to God's invitation has transformed world history. She had every reason to say no. For a young, unmarried woman (possibly a consecrated virgin), pregnancy posed serious challenges. Mary's response, "Behold, I am the handmaid of the Lord. May it be done to me according to your word" (Lk 1:38), is the posture all pilgrims strive for in their daily walk. Mary is the ideal because she lived this response throughout her life, always accepting what God had planned for her, silently reflecting on all the events of Jesus' life "in her heart" (Lk 2:19, 51). María's description of Mary's response is instructive:

> Mary's understanding of the Incarnation, like ours, unfolded over time. She continued to say yes to God at every step of living out the mystery, through the daily and ordinary events in life as well as through the major events as they evolved. When the angel Gabriel first appeared to her, Mary could not have imagined the passion and death of her Son. She knew that Jesus was destined for greatness, but she could not have known the cost—the agony of watching her son die. And even there, at the foot of the cross, in the greatest pain a mother can endure, Mary trusted that this mystery too would unfold as part of God's plan of salvation. There is nothing effortless about a mother who chooses to proclaim her faith in God while holding

the lifeless body of her son in her arms, the same child she once caressed and cradled when he was a baby. Yet this is the meaning of faith for a Christian, the call of a believer—to trust God, a good God who loves us and cares for us. *(The Seeker's Guide to Mary, pp. 33–34)*

The Pilgrimage We Share

Yes, Mary is the ideal. But, without looking too deeply into ourselves, we plainly see that we resemble Peter and the other apostles more than we do Mary. Jesus invites us to stay with him (Jn 1:39), and we truly desire to abandon everything to follow him (Mt 4:18–22). Through Peter, we know that Jesus is "the Messiah, the Son of the living God" (Mt 16:16). When Christ's teachings get tough, we want to answer, with Peter, "Master, to whom shall we go? You have the words of eternal life" (Jn 6:68). With the apostles and all the martyrs throughout church history, and without counting the cost, we want to live out the great commission, making disciples of all nations; baptizing them in the name of the Father, the Son, and the Holy Spirit; teaching them so that they too may live in communion with God forever.

We desire to desire. We desperately want to say yes to God's invitation. But, like Peter and the other apostles, we often fall desperately short. Like Peter, who initially rejected Christ's talk of passion and death, we often want to substitute our plans and wishes for God's will. Like the mother of James and John, who sought privileges for her sons, we are often tempted to put ourselves first. Like the apostles in the Garden of Gethsemane, we too often fall asleep when we should be keeping prayerful watch with

Christ. Like Peter after Jesus' arrest, we deny Christ daily every time we fail to see the face of Christ in our neighbor or in the mirror. Like the apostles after Jesus' death, we often lock the doors to our hearts out of fear, refusing to share our gifts with others.

Our inability to give an unqualified yes to Jesus reveals the true nature of our pilgrimage, which is to ask for the grace to surrender to God's will. Mary received this grace as a gift at the moment of her conception. For the rest of us, the whole history of salvation and the whole experience of our lives point to this one truth, which is captured in the Gospel by Peter's attempt to walk on water. In fear, after initially mistaking Jesus for a ghost, Peter said to Jesus, "'Lord, if it is you, command me to come to you on the water.' He said, 'Come.' Peter got out of the boat and began to walk on the water toward Jesus. But when he saw how (strong) the wind was he became frightened; and, beginning to sink, he cried out, 'Lord, save me!' Immediately Jesus stretched out his hand and caught him" (Mt 14:28–31). Lord, save me! Give me the strength to surrender my life to you and to serve you faithfully in this life by doing your will.

The end of our pilgrimage is eternal life with God. In John's Gospel, Jesus says, "[T]his is eternal life, that they should know you, the only true God, and the one whom you sent, Jesus Christ" (17:3). The *Catechism of the Catholic Church* (hereafter cited as "CCC") elaborates: "This perfect life with the Most Holy Trinity—this communion of life and love with the Trinity, with the Virgin Mary, the angels and all the blessed—is called 'heaven.' Heaven is the ultimate end and fulfillment of the deepest human longings, the state of supreme, definitive happiness" (1024). We can only progress along our pilgrimage to this point by crying out, with Peter, "Lord, save me!"

We have inherited the great pilgrimage of humanity. It is now our responsibility—our time in history—to respond to God's invitation. For each of us, there will be times when we say yes to God's invitation, but there will be many times when we, like the apostles, say no. Through it all, Christ walks with us, renewing the invitation. He gave us the church as his instrument of salvation. Through the church, he gave us his word in the form of tradition and Scripture. And he continually gives us his grace through the sacramental life. When we reject his call, he graces us with the sacrament of reconciliation. And to strengthen us for the journey, he gives us himself daily in the Eucharist. In 1996, on the Feast of Corpus Christi, Pope John Paul II gave his reflection titled *Eucharist: Sacrament of Human Pilgrimage*. We will give the Holy Father the final word in this chapter: "Christ the Eucharist guides the Church and all of us along the Way which is he himself, the Way that leads to the Father. . . . With your sacramental presence you give us a foretaste of the joy of complete and lasting participation in the Father's life at the eternal banquet."

The Companionship of Others' Prayers

In many different situations and in many different ways, other pilgrims join us on our journey through their prayers. At the Carmel of St. Joseph, located in Piedmont just northwest of Oklahoma City, a group of Discalced Carmelite Nuns quietly offer their prayers for the church and the world, day in and day out, year in and year out. Out of love for God and his people, they have responded to a call to step away from the crowds and pray. Although they remain in the convent, their prayers accompany those for whom they are offered. In 2003, Norman, Oklahoma, joined many other communities in perpetual adoration, a visible reminder that we journey home as One Body in Christ through the Eucharist we share. Around the clock—and across time, geography, and history—my brothers and sisters in faith unite their prayers with the body of believers by keeping a silent vigil before the Blessed Sacrament. One faithful woman in our parish prays daily at Mass for the Jacobs and D'Souza families. Another prays for the benefactors and clients of the local St. Vincent de Paul society. Together we offer prayers for the church, the nation, the sick, and the dead. All these prayers accompany the faithful.

Recently, I was talking with our pastor, Father Bill, about parish geographic boundaries, and he made the comment that the parish is responsible for all the souls within those boundaries. I knew that the parish had reciprocal responsibilities toward all its members, and I could see that it might possibly have responsibility for nonpracticing Catholics within its boundaries. But could it be that the local parish had some responsibility for the soul of every Protestant, Jew, Muslim, Hindu, Buddhist, agnostic, and atheist living within the parish boundaries? The comment startled me, but upon reflection, I could see that he was correct.

As inheritor of the great commission, the parish, through its members, has a responsibility to bring the gospel to the community, using words—as St. Francis once said—if it has to. And, as Christ's Body in a particular geographic location, the parish has a responsibility to offer prayers to the Father on behalf of all the souls within that area. Day in and day out, with much of the world oblivious to this sacred ritual, daily communicants offer their prayers on behalf of all in the community in the hope that their faith will not only aid themselves and the other faithful but also be instrumental in bringing lost and struggling souls to Christ's loving embrace. In this way, the parish imitates the crowd at Capernaum who brought a paralytic to Jesus: "Unable to get near Jesus because of the crowd, they opened up the roof above him. After they had broken through, they let down the mat on which the paralytic was lying. When Jesus saw *their* faith, he said to the paralytic, 'Child, your sins are forgiven'" (Mk 2:3–5, emphasis added). Daily, in an act of love for their neighbor, communicants are removing the roof and asking God to heal all the emotional and spiritual paralytics in the community.

Through our prayers, we join people who may not yet realize they are on a pilgrimage. Perhaps we are accompanying a paralytic to see Jesus. We may never know exactly how our prayers are manifested in the lives of people, but they are a way of being present to others.

The Companionship of the Saints

Catholics believe in the communion of saints. We journey with all of humanity—past, present, and future. In fact, the earth, along with all creation, is journeying from its origins toward a final destination. And as individuals whose lives unfold within the context of this larger drama, we experience our own earthly journeys from conception through birth to death. That journey can sometimes be easier when we remember that others have gone before us—and still, in a mysterious way, walk beside us.

Every year on November 1, we remember all the saints of the church who have successfully finished their pilgrim journey and who constitute a great cloud of witnesses interceding on our behalf as we continue our journey home to the Father. As the catechism says, the church canonizes some of these saints "by solemnly proclaiming that they practiced heroic virtue and lived in fidelity to God's grace." In this way, "the Church recognizes the power of the Spirit of holiness within her and sustains the hope of believers by proposing the saints to them as models and intercessors" (CCC 828).

St. Ignatius of Loyola:
A Journey in Patient Perseverance

Born in 1491, the young Ignatius found himself at court, where he seems to have indulged in some of the less virtuous "pleasures." He joined the army in 1517 and received a serious injury from a cannonball in 1521 while defending Pamplona from the French. Admiring his courage, the victorious French carried him back to his home in Loyola, where he would spend months recuperating.

During his convalescence, Ignatius asked for books of romance. Instead, he was given books on Christ and the saints. During this time, his imagination alternated between visions of chivalry and thoughts of saintly virtue. The secular thoughts left him dissatisfied, while the saintly ones gave him strength. His conversion was complete after a vision of Mary and the Christ child.

Ignatius persevered through the tribulations of war and wounds. But it was after his conversion that his real trials began. After a treacherous voyage to the Holy Land, he arrived only to be turned away by the Franciscans, who had charge of the holy sites. He returned to Spain to study but was thrown into jail on two occasions by interrogators of the Inquisition. He finished his studies in Paris. During his studies, Ignatius drew a following. His first two groups of followers deserted him, but the third group of six stayed with him as he formed the Society of Jesus (Jesuits) and put himself at the disposal of the pope.

Ignatius began developing what we now refer to as the Spiritual Exercises while in his early thirties. These exercises are still used as the basis for retreats and parish missions around the globe today. When he died in 1556, sixteen years after founding the Jesuits, the Society had grown to one thousand religious in a hundred houses. In 2001, a member of the Society, Avery Dulles, was named cardinal by Pope John Paul II.

Many of us might have abandoned the pilgrim path if faced with the obstacles confronting Ignatius. In times of trial, when we feel abandoned and alone, we can turn to him as one who, with God's grace, navigated his way to the great glory of God.

St. Elizabeth Ann Seton:
A Journey to the Catholic Faith

Mother Seton was the first American-born saint, canonized in 1975. She began life in 1774, the daughter of a prominent New York physician. She was married at nineteen by the local Episcopalian bishop and had five children. After her father-in-law and father died, her family fell into financial distress. To help relieve her husband's failing health, the family traveled to Italy, where her husband died.

In Italy, Elizabeth Ann Seton began attending Mass and grew to long for the Eucharist. Upon her return to the States, she gave serious consideration to becoming Catholic, even though doing so would weaken her financial position further because of the scandal it would cause her family. She was received into the church in 1805, followed by her sister-in-law a year later.

New York was an unfriendly place for this convert, and she considered moving to a convent in Canada, where she could teach and support her children. She ended up moving to Bishop John Carroll's diocese of Baltimore, where she opened schools for both the rich and the poor and she founded an order, the Sisters of Charity, based on the rule of the Sisters of Charity of St. Vincent de Paul. Soon, the Sisters of Charity spread across the continent, tending to the poor, the orphaned, and the sick.

When I begin to take the Catholic faith for granted, I remember those who paid a high price to journey into communion with us and how much they, like Elizabeth Seton, have given to Christ's Body by their faithful pilgrimage.

St. Teresa Benedicta of the Cross (Edith Stein):
A Journey to Truth and Meaning

Born on Yom Kippur—the Day of Atonement—in 1891, Edith Stein (the future St. Teresa Benedicta of the Cross) was the youngest of seven surviving children. Her father died when she was two, and she was raised by her devoutly

Jewish mother. Showing an independent streak from a young age, Edith made sure she started school a year earlier than she was supposed to, and then, at age fifteen, she quit. During her sabbatical from school at age fifteen, Edith had given up praying. As María wrote in her biography of Stein, *Edith Stein: St. Teresa Benedicta of the Cross*, it was unclear whether she was "an avowed atheist, a temporarily agnostic searcher, or a teenager testing her freedom" (p. 51).

Gifted intellectually and possessing a love of learning, Edith returned to school, earning a Ph.D. with highest honors in philosophy under Edmund Husserl, the founder of phenomenology. While studying philosophy, she began to appreciate Christianity, and after reading St. Teresa of Ávila's autobiography in one night, all her doubts were swept away.

As a woman and a Jew in Germany in the early years of the twentieth century, she found it difficult to obtain a teaching job at a university. Referred to as "the intellectual leader of Catholic feminism," she lectured, often on the nature and vocation of women. In 1932, she finally received a teaching post, only to be relieved of it a year later when Hitler came to power. She then fulfilled a decadelong dream and entered a Carmelite convent. She was killed in Auschwitz in 1942 and canonized in 1998.

Edith models the pilgrim's openness and inquisitiveness before the great questions of meaning and truth. Her search led her into the Catholic faith and brought her to embrace the cross in the midst of the Holocaust.

Karol Wojtyla:
A Journey to Community

Born in Poland in 1920, the aspiring young actor clandestinely began his seminary studies during the Nazi occupation. After study in Rome, the young priest returned to his native Poland in 1948, where he would spend the next thirty years tending his flock under the watchful eye of the atheistic Communist government.

Wujek ("Uncle"), as Father Wojtyla was called, was committed to proposing to the young that the Catholic Church had a better understanding of the human person and of history than did the Marxists. To accomplish this, he thoroughly immersed himself in the lives of his people, including their games and vacations. For twenty-five years, starting in 1953, he participated in an annual kayak trip with a large group that had grown up around him. Celebrating Mass in the open air, playing soccer, eating, praying, experiencing nature, and talking about every topic under the sun "was a form of ministry, a way of leading others to Christ," says Wojtyla's biographer George Weigel (*Witness to Hope*, p. 104).

Still alive and now well into the twenty-sixth year of his pontificate, Pope John Paul II remains a long way from being eligible for canonization. Yet we have little doubt that one day he will be referred to as St. John Paul the Great.

In reflecting on his life, we can look at his pilgrimage into a deep eucharistic communion with Christ and his church. We can also look at his pilgrimage toward unity of all Christians and toward full implementation of Vatican II. We can look to his pilgrimage with all people of goodwill as he gently proposes that freedom must once again be oriented toward truth—the truth about humanity and about God—if we are to throw off the tyranny of our culture of death and create a culture of life.

Companionship within Our Life Callings

God is a community of love: three in one. As creatures created in his image, we are called to live out our lives and our pilgrim journeys in the company of others. Most of us are called to walk the journey with one other person in marriage. Others are called to live the Christian pilgrimage in celibate religious life, as priests, sisters, and brothers. And still others are called to live that ideal in a single state.

María and I are called to live out this life as a married couple. Under the church's guidance, we wrote our own vows, and on December 27, 1981, we professed our love and commitment to each other in front of our Christian community at Our Lady Queen of Peace Chapel, promising each other, "Wherever you go I will go, wherever you lodge I will lodge, your people shall be my people, and your God my God." Of course, at twenty-one years of age, we didn't have a clue as to what we were getting ourselves into. We became "true yokemates" (Phil 4:3) that day, although we are on a lifetime journey to fully grasp what that means.

The catechism instructs us as to our vocation as a married couple: "Since God created him man and woman, their mutual love becomes an image of the absolute and unfailing love with which God loves man" (1604). We are called to be an image of "the absolute and unfailing love" of God. What an impossible task! Fortunately, we "have the strength for everything through him who empowers" us (Phil 4:13). God knows that it is impossible for us to fulfill our marital vocation on our own, so he pours sanctifying grace into this sacramental pilgrimage. The "grace proper to the sacrament of Matrimony is intended to perfect the couple's love and to strengthen their indissoluble unity. By this grace they 'help one another to attain holiness'" (CCC 1641).

María and I have found that we are yokemates to each other on our pilgrim journey on a number of levels. First, as male and female, Michael and María, we complement each other, each offering the gifts that the other lacks. Second, we support each other against the cold north wind that sometimes makes its way to Oklahoma in the form of disappointment or rejection. Third, we share the laughter and the tears of a life lived together raising four children. But primarily, we help each other attain holiness by the constant call to die to ourselves as we put the needs of the other first.

The call to give completely to our spouse in perfect freedom mirroring the Trinity's eternal self-giving is God's unique way of helping us surrender to him and thus advance on our journey. I learned this the hard way. In the spring of 1989, I was offered a position as an associate professor of law at the University of Oklahoma. I desperately wanted to take the job. I had grown up in a college town with a father who taught economics, and I thought this life provided an ideal setting for raising children. The academic life of thinking, teaching, and writing also appealed to me. I was also miserable in my law firm. The work didn't excite me much, and the hours were brutal on family life. And my boss wanted even more hours from me. I felt I was withering on the vine in that environment.

There was only one problem. At the time, we lived not in Norman, Oklahoma, but in Austin, Texas. And María didn't want to move. She rightly questioned my long-term commitment to this latest desire. After all, only a few years earlier, I had tilted at windmills, moving the family to Washington, D.C., in fulfillment of a youthful fantasy, only to return to Austin a year later. By 1989, we had children in school; it was time to end these childlike quests and settle down. We also had family and good friends in Austin. With these people, we had celebrated

church is subordinate to Christ, so wives should be subordinate to their husbands in everything" (Eph 5:22–24).

María was devastated. Her devastation did not arise out of our impending move, however. Her hurt and anger grew out of my betrayal of our marriage vows. She knew a truth that would take me years to comprehend. She kept this secret to herself, knowing that it was something I had to discover for myself. I still marvel at her patience. She was graced with the wisdom to know that *telling* me the truth might only delay by months or years my ability to *hear* the truth. I had betrayed our marriage vows by abusing the Scripture. I wielded Ephesians 5 as a source of power. Was this a Christlike action? In my attempt to rationalize my decision, I hadn't looked very closely at that part of Scripture. My heart's eye had not focused on verse 21: "Be subordinate to one another out of reverence for Christ." I also had failed to adequately reflect on verses 25–28: "Husbands, love your wives, even as Christ loved the church and handed himself over for her to sanctify her . . . that she might be holy and without blemish. So (also) husbands should love their wives as their own bodies. He who loves his wife loves himself."

Ephesians 5 is not about power but about surrender and the giving of oneself fully to another. It is within marriage that we learn self-giving and begin to mirror, however inadequately, the Father's eternal love for the Son and the Son's eternal love for the Father. I failed that day in a big way. María knew it, but instead of abandoning me, she waited patiently for God to move in my life so that I could be healed and our marriage could be solidified.

My betrayal raised immediate logistical questions. María simply told me that she and the children were not going to make the move in the autumn of 1989 and that I could make the five-hour commute between Austin and

Norman weekly. It was my turn to be devastated. I had just finished constructing *my* ideal life for our family, and my wife wasn't buying into it. I thought she had ruined my life. At the time, I thought she had betrayed me, but looking back on it, I see that she was the ever-faithful spouse, remaining committed to our marriage while letting me suffer the consequences of my actions.

During four years of commuting, I stayed in Norman only one weekend. The first two years were extremely difficult emotionally and spiritually. Although we remained committed to our marriage vows, we didn't like each other much during that time. Years later, in an article about this period in our lives, María wrote, "I could hear my insides saying, 'I give up. I am tired of fighting. I am tired of trying to talk—only to end up in screams, or worse, cold stares. I am tired of lying next to a stranger at night, tired of living in separate worlds under the same roof" ("From Ashes to Easter," p. 16)."

As tired and frustrated as she was, she didn't give up. Instead, she "committed to prayer like never before" (p. 17). As she wrote, "I sat quietly, daily dropping all my anger before the Lord rather than flinging it at Michael. I waited, knowing that nothing that could happen at this time was in my hands. Only God could right the wrongs. I simply, honestly, humbly said, 'yes'—to whatever was to happen" (p. 17).

My life had to come crashing down in a ruined heap of dreams turned to nightmares before I could wake and truly start living. The pilgrimage road is about surrender, an emptying of self so that God can bestow blessing beyond imagination. I wish that I could have followed Christ's example and given myself fully to God and my wife without the pain caused by my abuse of power. But God is merciful and follows even the wayward on their journeys. As I drove up and down Interstate 35 between

Austin and Norman in an old Subaru wagon, God began to work on me. Knowing that I am a slow study, I am thankful that he had patience as this highway became a metaphor for my journey. At first, I was mad at María for not playing along with my decision. Then, for the first time in my life, I got mad at God for his cruel joke of setting me up in a picturesque life only to destroy it before it began.

One night as I was driving back to Norman, I finally surrendered, saying:

> Lord, I don't know what you have in mind for me—for us. I know that you brought María and me together. I believe in and am committed to our sacred marriage. I don't know how our living and working situation will resolve itself, but that is none of my concern. María and I are on a lifelong journey together, and we are at a point in the trip where it is dark outside, with snow or rain further limiting our visibility and making the way slick and hazardous. Even if I can't see one foot in front of my face, I trust that you will lead us.

For the first time in my life, I held nothing back when I said, "Thy will be done." I was completely impoverished, having lost my concept of work, family, and even God himself, and I was now ready to turn my life completely over to God. With my heart softened, I began—emphasis on *began*—to see the error of my ways. And, over the next two years, our marital relationship started to heal.

I had long since stopped asking María if and when she would be moving to Norman. Then, unexpectedly, during a spring break breakfast in 1993, María said that she and the kids would be joining me in Norman that fall. Her hesitation about moving had never been about the move itself; it had been about my betrayal and abuse of position. As our relationship healed, she once again demonstrated her love by moving. I have no idea what blessings would have been bestowed upon us if I hadn't misused Scripture to assert my authority. But I do know that God is faithful and has nevertheless tremendously blessed our lives these past ten years.

I now see that a key to learning how to love God and allow myself to be loved by God is to love my wife and allow myself to be loved by her. God has given me an incredible yokemate as a companion for the journey. But in a very real way, for me, María *is* the journey.

I am not a poet, but for some reason I penned the following in my travel journal last summer:

> Two bodies entangled in love
> Husband and Wife—two bodies one flesh.
> Three persons entangled in love
> Nay, three persons are Love
> Father, Son, and Spirit—our Holy Trinity blessed.

Authentic love between the husband and wife expands out from itself. As the catechism says, "The Christian family is a communion of persons, a sign and image of the communion of the Father and the Son in the Holy Spirit" (CCC 2205). Marriage, like religious life, is "directed towards the salvation of others; if [it contributes] as well to personal salvation, it is through service to others that [it does] so" (ibid., 1534).

I have shared intimately with you some of our walk as companions in marriage in the hope that our story will help you see the profound nature of the pilgrimage. Because we got married at the ripe old age of twenty-one (we tell our children, "Do as I say, not as I do!"), we don't have much experience in living life in a single state, although we each have a brother who is in his forties and single. We also haven't experienced religious or ordained life firsthand, but we have been fortunate to have been befriended by several religious throughout our lives.

On a pastoral visit to Australia in 1986, the pope said that "single people who love Christ with a chaste and generous heart have their own gifts to bring to parish life. Since they do not have the daily obligations of a husband or wife and children, they often have opportunities to help both Church and society in general. Their own experience of single life can make them especially aware of those who are often forgotten and overlooked by society" (Address of John Paul II to in St. Leo Parish, Paragraph 5, Melbourne, Australia, November 28, 1986).

As the Holy Father suggests, single life has its own special burdens because the life of the parish and the life of society are often organized around families and children. An unmarried person can feel like the odd person out. Because of this, singles sometimes have to work harder to fit in. The pope suggests an important vocation for singles. Precisely because they may be overlooked and forgotten, Christians who are single can walk in solidarity (at least in prayer) with the world's truly forgotten.

The pope also suggests that without primary familial obligations, the single person can be Christ to the world in ways that parents and husbands or wives cannot. We have witnessed this in the lives of Greg (my brother) and Ignacio (María's brother). Both have been remarkable uncles, spending time with our children in ways that other siblings can't.

Ignacio, a high-school teacher, immerses himself in the lives of his students. He is able to integrate faith and learning because he sees many of the same students in his work with the youth at his parish. Greg has the gift of presence. He takes time to be present to old friends in a way that this father of four can only dream of. And he annually wins the "neighbor of the year" award for making sure that others in his area feel welcome. Ignacio and Greg, living out their pilgrim lives in the single state, provide examples of community consciousness in a culture that is becoming more and more geared to the individual.

By the nature of the office, companionship in ministerial priesthood is unique. The catechism teaches that "priests share in the universal dimensions of the mission that Christ entrusted to the apostles" (1565). They are ordained "not for a limited and restricted mission, 'but for the fullest, in fact the universal mission of salvation "to the end of the earth"'" (ibid.). They preach, they shepherd, and they bring the bread of life to hungry pilgrims. I must be a companion primarily to my wife, but the ordained priests cannot limit their companionship in this way.

Priests need companions who will befriend and strengthen them as they act as companions for all of us on our pilgrimage. My sense is that with more and more parishes staffed by only one priest, many priests live alone. Additionally, pastors are often encumbered by an emotional distance between themselves and their parishes. With these built-in obstacles, it is imperative that the priest seek intimate companionship in prayer with God. Intimate human relationships are also necessary because each of us needs "God in the skin"—to love and to be loved concretely and not just in abstract communal settings. Our priests are human like the rest of us, and just as I needed to be held accountable in my marriage, our priests need to be held accountable for their attitudes and actions and to be corrected on occasion.

Like priests, others living a professed religious life (such as brothers and sisters) are called to accompany us on our pilgrim journey "as a special sign of the mystery of redemption" (CCC 932). Because they "follow and imitate Christ more nearly and . . . manifest more clearly his self-emptying," they "encourage their brethren by their example," bearing "striking witness 'that the world cannot be transfigured and offered to God without the spirit of the beatitudes'" (ibid.).

María and I have had our lives enriched in numerous ways by our many friends who have dedicated their lives to Christ by entering the religious life. Some, like Paulist Father Bruce Neili, are tremendous preachers whose words grip those in the pew and turn them back to the pilgrim path. Others, like Sister Tess Browne, have witnessed to me by devoting their lives to the poor and the marginalized. Others, like Benedictine Brother Kevin McGuire, remind us by their gentle spirit that all life is grace. Last year, we traveled to Parsons, Kansas, to attend the celebration marking Father Charles Miller's fiftieth anniversary as a Marianist. The community of faith can only begin to thank Father Charles for fifty years of educating young college students, proposing—in an intellectually rigorous way—the reasonableness of a Christian worldview in the face of the secular alternatives. And we are forever indebted to Father Bill Dougherty, who, by God's grace, showed up on our doorstep just as María and I were entering the dark night of our marriage.

Whether we are single, religious, or married, we are called to love our neighbor as ourselves, each living a life of loving service to others according to his or her unique call, circumstances, and vocation. The cloistered nuns in Piedmont, Oklahoma, and even the hermits who live alone in the desert serve by praying without ceasing on behalf of all God's creatures. Lawyers, doctors, nurses, accountants, CEOs, janitors, garbage collectors, fathers, mothers, and children all serve in their own unique ways.

Companionship of Those Who Arrive Unexpectedly

All kinds of people present themselves in our lives. Sometimes we see them as irritations because they drain our precious time or because they have annoying habits or mannerisms. Sometimes we see them as opportunities to advance our own agendas because they are people of influence and power. Sometimes we are hesitant to receive them because of a history of hurts and slights. How often do we choose to view the people who cross our paths as gifts given to us by our loving Father? How often do we treat them as if they were Christ himself?

One of my first experiences of confronting an unexpected and unwelcome companion occurred during my freshman year of college. Living at a fraternity house in the same town as my parents, I had frequent contact with them, most notably when my clothes were dirty. One day that spring, my dad called to ask me a favor. At our pastor's request, he had taken in a homeless man who needed a place to stay for three or four days until a government check arrived in the mail. Because my three sisters were living at home, my dad was uncomfortable with a stranger staying at our house, and he wondered if I could take him in. How could I do this? I was only a pledge—not even a full member of the fraternity. I was sure the man would have long, dirty hair and would smell terrible. (It turned out to be worse than I thought.) I don't know why I said yes, but I learned a valuable lesson when I introduced this man to my fraternity brothers as my friend and guest. I learned that—at least this once—I had the courage to treat another human being as Christ might have, even if it meant possible ridicule and scorn from people I'd been trying to impress.

As we mention in the acknowledgments, our son, Christopher, traveled the country as part of NET Ministries, which promotes youth evangelization. During that time, he gave retreats for high-school and junior-high-school students. We became acquainted with NET when Chris was in sixth grade and attended a NET retreat. That year, we hosted some of the NET team members in our house, and we have hosted teams every year since. It can be a lot of work—setting up beds and doing extra cooking and cleaning. But no matter how tired or distracted we are, we have found it to be worth hosting NET team members in our home. Every year, the team members renew our family with their youthful passion for the Lord. I remember distinctly the first year we hosted NET: Two young people stood in our kitchen excitedly sharing their love of the Eucharist with our son. And he was gobbling it up. What more could we ask from these strangers who had shattered our routine?

For several years, we have hosted a high-school (and now college) New Year's Eve party. Imagine dozens of people dancing to the Beatles in the living room or playing foosball or darts in the game room. New Year's Eve 2001 was cold and icy in Norman, Oklahoma. At 2 A.M., we discovered that all the cars had been covered with eggs. So instead of heading off to bed, I went to the car wash with the partygoers to help them clean off their cars. We learned who the perpetrator was fairly quickly—a young woman who thought she wasn't invited because we hadn't issued her a personal invitation. Three months later, she appeared on our doorstep to apologize and ask our forgiveness. She is now a regular at our house and doesn't wait for a formal invitation. We saw firsthand why the pope places so much hope in this generation of young people as we witnessed her courage in coming forward uncoerced. We think she learned a lesson in love and forgiveness. And the incident has now receded far enough into the past that we can all laugh about it now.

Unexpected companions can bring lighthearted and totally unexpected joy to our lives. This past year, we shared our Easter meal with three college students who were not traveling home for the weekend. We asked our children if they minded sharing our traditional Easter egg hunt with our guests. The kids agreed it was okay, and María and I prepared a few more eggs. What we didn't know was that one of our guests, a twenty-two-year-old, had never hunted for eggs before. Her enthusiasm returned us momentarily to a sense of childhood innocence.

Who are our companions on the journey? Those who pray for us. Those who have gone before us. Those who share in our vocation. And those we never expected. Whether we journey through a sacramental relationship or events over which we have no control, God will always make sure that other pilgrims are close by.

6

Getting Help
for the Interior Journey

~ María ~

I have been on the move all my life. And my understanding of pilgrimage has developed over many years and experiences. Because I was raised in a Cuban Catholic home, my understanding has been influenced by my ethnicity and by the condition of growing up as an immigrant and a refugee. From early on, I understood pilgrimage as some form of religious journey that incorporated aspects of both piety and spirituality. Yet as the only daughter in a refugee family, my vision presupposed an element of sacrifice as well—a cost, a payment, some kind of human suffering. Even if I couldn't quite name the effects of such habitual moving and changing schools, I felt as if life itself was a painful pilgrimage with a cost much too high to pay. As I grew older, I resented the requirement that life seemed to make of me—to always be on the move, without a sense of permanence or belonging—and pilgrimage felt more like a burden than a blessing.

In my adult life, I have traveled professionally as a journalist for the Catholic press, often reporting on some kind of tragedy or catastrophic situation: children living in the trash dumps in Haiti; the horrors of the 1995 Oklahoma City bombing; the struggle for survival of Palestinian Christians living in Israel; the tragic mudslides in Honduras following Hurricane Mitch in 1999. On the one hand, these professional trips seemed to reinforce my personal view that suffering was a required cost of our pilgrimage through life. Slowly but persistently, these tragedies and life-threatening circumstances also exposed me to the grace of faith in the middle of tragedy and of hope in the midst of despair. Over the years, these traveling experiences that were part of my professional life began an inner transformation of my vision of pilgrimage. Suffering does not by itself a pilgrimage make; sometimes suffering is not even the key aspect of sacred travel. I now understand that a change—surrender, growth—must take place inside me, and that transformation is what turns a mere journey into a pilgrimage.

In each one of my experiences, the actual physical journey, the people, and even the situation that I encountered, all became conduits for a transformation of some sort within me—or at least, they were the agents for an *invitation* to grow.

Obviously, we cannot *make* a transformation happen within us, no matter how much we want it or how hard we try. The pilgrimage journey is about surrendering our will, fears, desires, and hopes to the one whom we claim as the center of life. But because of the human condition, we cannot make this change happen. We cannot force or speed up the process. As the psalmist says, we "wait with longing for the Lord" (Ps 130:5), in trust and confidence that his love will bring us home.

There are some things, however, that we can do consciously to embrace a posture of openness in our waiting. There are actions we can take when we travel that make us more accessible to the blessings and graces God has in mind for us. There are travel tools that can improve and nourish our sensitivity and our level of awareness so that we will be able to see and hear God in the experiences of the journey. There are ways to discipline ourselves to become conscious of the light already present in each moment. And we do all of this, even as we wait for the Lord, in the hope that we will become ever more aware that we are traveling together toward the one God who is always calling us home.

Journal Keeping

Journaling is a primary tool for the pilgrimage journey. I have always played around with writing. As a child in grade school, I could pour into a poem emotions that I could not yet name. My parents still have this collection of sappy yet honest Spanish poems that reflect not only who I was emotionally but who I wanted to become. Like nothing else, writing has always called forth honesty from my deepest self. When I write, not only do I open my heart to the truths of this moment, but at times, I touch a well of wisdom that I have learned to humbly recognize as the Holy Spirit within me. I have learned that writing parallels and mirrors my spiritual life. It allows me to name, in a sense, where I am in the spiritual journey.

I keep several different journals at a time. Every morning I write three "morning pages," allowing whatever comes to mind to be put on paper. At times, this practice serves as a sort of kick start to my writing. Other times, it feels more like a purging that I need to go through before

I get to the "real" stuff, the well itself, like clearing the desk of papers before you can begin to work or like picking up all the things from the floor before you can get a sense of what the room looks like.

I also have a journal that functions as an album of ideas, images, and quotes that have inspired me. I cite several quotes from a book that I may be reading and then write my thoughts about them. Or I may write down an idea for a story, perhaps a character description or a story line that I find exciting. Or I attempt to draw a picture of an experience or an event that moved me, as I did after watching the stunning Leonid meteor shower from our backyard at 4 A.M. I wanted to somehow capture what my daughter Michelle and I saw. I wanted to record the explosion of light in the dark sky and the gut reaction that we had as we spontaneously said, "Oohh" and "Aahh"—much in the same manner that we do when watching fireworks on the Fourth of July. I am *not* a good artist, but it was much fun to give color to that experience, to play with shades of light and dark in my journal. It was a delight to try to capture our feelings on paper using something other than words.

As you would expect, I also keep a "regular" journal, the type in which I list dates and tell about my day, my thoughts and feelings. But I also include in this journal "aha" moments, those testaments of grace when God reminds me of a truth that my heart has always known. I journal about my dreams, what I remember of them, especially what feelings prevailed during my dream and as I woke up. I journal about my prayer experience and my struggles with the methods of prayer, but also about the insights and awareness that motivate and guide my daily pilgrimage.

When our family first learned about my mom's colon cancer, we were compelled to go on yet another pilgrimage. I felt the need to write down every nuance of that experience. When I came home from a chemotherapy session or a visit to the hospital, I would start writing; it was like a cleansing shower after a workout. During this period, I noted in my journal:

> There is a nurse at the doctor's office whose care and compassion for Mom and for the other patients is deep and evident. When Tori comes to connect her to the IV, she brings her rollaway chair as close to Mom as she can, and she touches Mom's arms softly, tenderly, as if her skin were the softest material she's ever felt. She is looking for a good vein, which at this point [in the chemotherapy] is hard to find. The last two times she's been "lucky," she said, and she was able to find a vein on her first stick. When she doesn't get it, she apologizes to Mom with such feeling, truly aware that every little pain only increases the big pains. It's not that we feel less when things get bigger; it's rather that we feel more. We feel everything, especially when it comes to pain. Every experience of pain makes us less willing, more fearful, which is why feeling and loving become more deliberate choices.

During those long months, I wanted—and needed—to write down every detail that I noticed, about the doctor, about the room, about the foreign medical lingo that the medical professionals used and expected us to understand. I wanted to record my emotions, though I often had no clue how to label the tornado of feelings whirling inside me. I wanted to pray, on paper, what I couldn't pray out loud. Sometimes I needed to fight with God. But more often I simply needed to write on paper what it felt like to mourn the fact that my mother was no longer the woman I remembered. Even as I sat beside her and listened to her breathe, I knew that I was watching my mother die. I couldn't say those things out loud, so I wrote them. I didn't want to just survive through that year and a half of surgery and chemotherapy; I wanted it to become a true pilgrimage of whatever God was showing me, telling me, through my mom's experience. And journaling became a fundamental tool in this process.

When I travel, whether with the family or alone, I use a journal to write down how I feel, what I have experienced in my day. I write down conversations that I've had with people in my group or with perfect strangers. I record details that I want to remember or that strike me as significant. When we were in Rome, for example, I recorded our visit to Santa Maria di Trastevere, site of one of the oldest communities in Rome and the community to whom Paul addressed his letters (now in the Bible as the book of Romans). This impressive historical fact moved me beyond words as we stood at that church and touched the wall filled with pieces of stone from the first century. I felt united through time and space with the saints and martyrs that came before us. Later that afternoon, sitting on the steps of the fountain in the Piazza di Trastevere, we ate what everyone in our family voted was the best pizza we'd had during our whole stay in Italy. A few days later, I also noted in my journal the name of the town where we switched trains as we left Rome—Terontola—a nondescript place where we waited for an hour and a half for our next train, to Assisi. More important, however, I described a scene that I inadvertently witnessed. It was a simple, tender moment between our oldest daughter, Anamaría, and her two sisters as she clearly played "big sister" exploring the edge of the town. Even the memory of that image makes me smile. It was an ordinary and momentous moment of grace.

When writing in a journal, there is no wrong way of doing things. Whether traveling or recording a slice of daily life, it isn't so much the facts involved that are essential; it is your observations and reactions to each particular situation that are significant. Something about writing it all down, including the process itself, clears the connection between the details seen by your eyes and the truths recognized by your heart. What is truly important is that writing it down and reading it years later become reminders of a moment in your life, a specific instant during your trip, when you became aware of the presence of grace. Writing is a way of seeing, not of saying. God is always there, whether we acknowledge him or not. But as we become aware, we recognize those moments of grace more and more frequently. A journal is a wonderful way to record those moments and to be reminded of the blessings, present every day, as we learn to recognize them on every journey.

The Way of the Cross

There are certain prayer devotions that, by their form and their essence, promote a sense of spiritual awareness and make us better pilgrims.

The object of the way of the cross (also known as the stations of the cross) is to help us make a pilgrimage, in spirit, to the most important scenes in the story of Christ's suffering and death. In a very real sense, the way of the cross constitutes a miniature pilgrimage to Jerusalem and to the holy places that marked the passion and death of Jesus. Or perhaps more accurately, it is a prayerful pilgrimage to the holy *moments* of Jesus' journey to Calvary. The stations of the cross consist of fourteen markers (or "stations") depicting a particular scene or moment, represented in some visual form to allow an individual or a group to literally walk, and meditate on, Jesus' journey. This form of reflecting on Christ's passion is an ancient tradition in the church. Although not called by this name before the sixteenth century, the actual Via Dolorosa ("Way of Suffering") in Jerusalem "was reverently marked out from the earliest times and has been the goal of pious pilgrims ever since the days of Constantine" (*Catholic Encyclopedia*, under "Way of the Cross"). The emergence of the stations of the cross as a devotion reflected the "desire to reproduce the holy places in other lands, in order to satisfy the devotion of those who were hindered from making the actual pilgrimage, [which] seems to have manifested itself at quite an early date" (ibid.).

One of our family's favorite Holy Week devotions is to walk the way of the cross at 3 P.M. on Good Friday, the hour that Scripture notes Christ died on the cross. When our young family lived in Annandale, Virginia, our parish held stations on Good Friday at the old St. Mary's Church, a small wooden chapel where Clara Barton had once tended to the wounded during the Civil War. The most meaningful aspect of the stations there, however, was that they were held outside, in the cemetery behind the old church. There was something not only appropriate but also proper about this setting, and even at the ages of four and two, our children recognized the sacredness of these circumstances. Years later, we continued this Good Friday tradition at our parish in Austin, Texas, even taking the children out of school early to walk and pray the stations together. Stations of the cross at St. Thomas More Parish took place in a beautiful outdoor garden made of indigenous rocks, with a path that swerved around clumps of cedar trees, which are native and plentiful in the Texas hill country.

But perhaps the most moving way of the cross for me over the years has been the one hosted on Holy Week at our current parish, also St. Thomas More, in Norman, Oklahoma. Because we are a university parish and a student center, every Good Friday, the community gathers for the way of the cross on the University of Oklahoma campus. Parishioners of all ages, from children to college students and older folks, take turns carrying a life-size wooden cross through the college campus. As our group prays through the stations of the cross, we stop at specific places on campus to recite a meditation that not only recalls the story of our Lord's passion but also reflects on its application to our daily lives. Inevitably, as the group progresses from the university's main building to the library, to the north oval, to the student union, and on to other campus sites, people spontaneously join us as we walk—many of them are simply attracted by the cross and the quiet, solemn procession through campus. Although we've never had a disruptive scene, we have always encountered a few jeerers or people making fun of such a public display of faith. But as I have reminded our children over the years, this, too, helps us to remember Jesus' Good Friday experience as he humbly walked through the crowded streets of Jerusalem, carrying his cross to the hill at Golgotha.

Although it is an integral part of most parishes during Lent and Holy Week celebrations, the way of the cross is not an activity restricted to the Lenten season. Clearly one of the most popular of Catholic devotions, the way of the cross is "said," or prayed, by passing from one station to the next, with certain prayers and a meditation recited at each stop or image. It is also common to recite or sing a verse from a song between one station and the next. Although the exact number of stations has varied considerably over the years and in different places of the world, fourteen stations is the norm (a fifteenth station is sometimes added to include the resurrection of Jesus):

1. Jesus is condemned to death.

2. Jesus is given his cross.

3. Jesus falls the first time.

4. Jesus meets his mother.

5. Simon of Cyrene helps Jesus.

6. Veronica cleanses the face of Jesus.

7. Jesus falls the second time.

8. Jesus meets the women of Jerusalem.

9. Jesus falls the third time.

10. Jesus is stripped of his clothing.

11. Jesus is nailed to the cross.

12. Jesus dies on the cross.

13. Jesus is taken down from the cross.

14. Jesus is placed in the tomb.

According to the *Catholic Encyclopedia* (under "Way of the Cross"), a group of connected chapels intended to represent the more important shrines in Jerusalem was constructed as early as the fifth century by St. Petronius, bishop of Bologna, Italy. These chapels "may perhaps be regarded as the germ from which the Stations afterwards developed, though it is tolerably certain that nothing that we have before about the fifteenth century can strictly be called a Way of the Cross in the modern sense" (ibid.). The definition of what constituted the way of the cross emerged as a consequence of strong devotion to the passion of Jesus during the twelfth and thirteenth centuries. Although the stations of the cross did not become a general church devotion before the end of the seventeenth century, the fourteen stations that make up the way of the cross are now found in every Catholic church.

Today, as throughout history, people who are unable to make the pilgrimage to Jerusalem and walk where Jesus literally walked can nevertheless make the pilgrimage of his passion in churches and retreat centers all over the world.

A few years ago, I traveled for my annual retreat to the Spiritual Life Center in Wichita, Kansas, about two hours north of our home in Norman, Oklahoma. On the third day, my afternoon walk took me from the adjacent diocesan cemetery to a lovely outdoor garden path that culminated in an impressive set of outdoor stations of the cross, brass-colored three-dimensional tablets set on large pieces of white sandstone.

I don't know what drew me to walk the stations of the cross that July afternoon. It was a fiery 101-degree day. I didn't have any books or materials to lead me through meditations for each station. Nor do I make a practice of regularly doing this spiritual devotion, let alone doing it by myself. I simply began to walk the path already before me, stopping at every image and reading the name of each station out loud. As I stopped at the ninth station, I was stumped by the rendering before me. It was as if I had never before seen that image—Jesus falling for the third time. At least, I had never seen it like this. There was Jesus, the Son of God, with a cross so heavy on his body that he didn't just stumble; he was forced prostrate on the dirty ground, with the weight of the wood across his wounded back. So much about that three-dimensional representation deeply touched me. The suffering. The weight. The depth of faithfulness. The profound love. I could suddenly see, with a fresh understanding, just how much Jesus loved us. As I stood before this image, then knelt in awe before it, I heard and saw in my heart how much Jesus, the Son of God, *already* loved me, personally. No matter what I do or don't do, he already loved me— enough to fall three times as he carried the weight of the cross, enough to die for me.

In his book *Border of Death, Valley of Life: An Immigrant Journey of Heart and Spirit*, Holy Cross Father Daniel G. Groody describes the life of undocumented immigrants in the United States as a contemporary Golgotha experience. "The journey across the border of death is a very real way of the cross for many immigrants, and the entrance to the United States is an experience of crucifixion," notes Groody, who says it can also be the place where some experience the rising to a new life (p. 33). Explaining the plight of undocumented Mexican immigrants, he writes:

> [They experience] nothing short of a walk across a border of death. Even when they do not die physically, they undergo a death culturally, psychologically, socially, and emotionally. . . . The Mexican immigrant experiences an agonizing movement from belonging to nonbelonging, from relational connectedness to family separation, from being to non-being, from life to death. . . . These immigrants are willing to descend into the depths of hell in the desert for the people they love so that they

may have better lives. Within their particular
stories of hunger, thirst, estrangement, nakedness,
sickness, and imprisonment, we can begin to see
the face of a crucified Christ (Mt 25:31–26:2). In
their suffering, the immigrants reveal the hidden
mystery of Christ today. (pp. 32–33)

So we see that people continue to walk the way of the
cross in many forms. As we make our own journeys, we will
encounter other pilgrims, and each one has a story. Often
that person's journey is yet another interpretation of the
journey our Lord has already made.

Whether in a church setting, on a college campus, or
even as a self-designed path through your backyard or neighborhood, praying through the way of the cross can be an
important tool for the faith journey. Besides the obvious
benefits of meditating on the actual story of Jesus' passion
and death, and on God's great love for each of us, the ultimate purpose of the way of the cross is to open our hearts to
a new understanding of God as present in our world today.

The Rosary

Like the way of the cross, the rosary is a form of mental
and vocal prayer; it is centered on events in the lives of
Jesus and his mother, Mary. In much the same way that a
stained-glass window in a church invites us to meditate on
God by presenting a moment in the life of Christ or a picture of a saint, the rosary uses our fingers and our lips to
invite our hearts to recall and meditate on Scripture.

The rosary is meant to encourage introspection and
reflection through meditation and repetition. Although
this tradition was shaped by devotion to Mary, the rosary
remains a Christ-centered prayer. All the prayers of the

rosary are found in the Scriptures. This is also true of the twenty familiar events in the lives of Jesus and Mary that serve as meditation for each "decade" of the rosary (a decade is a set of ten Hail Marys). To recite or to pray the rosary is to meditate on familiar stories of the Christian history of salvation. In the rosary, these stories are divided into four sets (joyful, luminous, sorrowful, and glorious) of five "mysteries," or specific moments in the life of Jesus or Mary:

The Joyful Mysteries

The Annunciation
The Visitation
The Nativity
The presentation of Jesus in the temple
Finding the child Jesus in the temple

The Luminous Mysteries

The baptism in the Jordan
The wedding at Cana
The proclamation of the kingdom
The Transfiguration
The first Eucharist

The Sorrowful Mysteries

The agony in the garden
The scourging at the pillar
The crowning with thorns
The carrying of the cross
The Crucifixion

The Glorious Mysteries

The Resurrection

The Ascension

The descent of the Holy Spirit upon the apostles

The Assumption

The coronation of Mary

Because "no one knows Christ better than Mary," as Pope John Paul II pointed out in his apostolic letter "The Rosary of the Virgin Mary," "no one can introduce us to a profound knowledge of his mystery better than his Mother. . . . Contemplating the scenes of the Rosary in union with Mary is a means of learning from her to 'read' Christ, to discover his secrets and to understand his message. . . . As we contemplate each mystery of her Son's life, she invites us to do as she did at the Annunciation: to ask humbly the questions which open us to the light, in order to end with the obedience of faith: 'Behold I am the handmaid of the Lord; be it done to me according to your word' (Lk 1:38)."

The religious exercise of reciting prayers while following a string of beads or a knotted cord is widespread among the major religious groups, occurring not only in the Christian tradition but also in Hinduism, Buddhism, and Islam. One of the most ancient prayer forms, the practice apparently originated in the early days of Christianity among monks and hermits, who would use a piece of heavy cord knotted at intervals as they recited their shorter prayers.

A few years ago, Michael shared with me that he had taken up the practice of saying the rosary on the twenty-five-minute drive to pick up or drop off our children at school each day. Then I, too, adopted the practice. When we do this, the rosary becomes a meditative tool that helps us to pray without ceasing and in all circumstances. The rosary also suggests that by meditating on specific moments in the life of Jesus—such as the Nativity, Jesus' presentation in the temple, Mary and Joseph's finding Jesus in the temple after three days—we bring the gospel into the mundane moments of daily life: What does Jesus' presentation in the temple mean to me as a pilgrim? How does the reality of Jesus' birth change my life today? Do I join Mary and Joseph in looking for Jesus? Where do I find him?

In my adult life, the rosary has also become a form of intercessory prayer. I have learned to recognize moments when a person comes to mind or when I wake up during the night with thoughts about a particular person as an invitation to pray for that person. Quite often, I don't pray the whole rosary, but rather, I offer a decade for that person whom the Holy Spirit has brought to my awareness. By doing so, I lift up that particular person's needs and intentions as a bouquet of prayers for my friend, putting her in the hands of the one who knows and loves her best. Praying the rosary reminds me that we walk this pilgrimage of faith as a *community* of Christian believers.

We have prayed the rosary on our travels and in the course of physical pilgrimages. This pilgrimage aid has helped us most consistently on our daily journeys through work, school, community involvement, and life at home. It helps us attach even our mundane tasks to Jesus' life and the holy purposes to which he has called us.

The Labyrinth

On our twenty-first anniversary, Michael and I together walked the brand-new outdoor labyrinth in Norman, Oklahoma. Built as a permanent memorial to the victims of the attacks of September 11, 2001, the Norman labyrinth was named the "Prairie Peace Path," and it is located in one of the city's largest parks. The Norman labyrinth is fashioned after historical Cretan designs; it is sixty-five feet in diameter and has seven circuits. Its defining boundaries are made from native Oklahoma granite. It was our first time to walk the labyrinth together as a prayer experience, and it was Michael's first time to walk a labyrinth at all. It's nice to know that after twenty-one years, we can still discover new ways to pray together as a couple—as well as new methods to enhance our under-standing of marriage as a pilgrimage. I was especially moved that day to find at the center of this labyrinth a tree of ribbons, with written prayers and wishes left there by individuals who had walked before us.

Labyrinths have long been used as tools for meditation and prayer. A labyrinth is not a maze or a puzzle to be solved. It does not require logical, sequential, analytical activity aimed at finding a correct path. A labyrinth is uni-cursal; that is, it has only one path. The way in is also the way out. There is no right or wrong way to walk a labyrinth. You can walk as fast or as slowly as you want. You can stop along the way or dance your way through the path. Once at the center, you can stay as long as you want before following the same path to walk out. A labyrinth involves intuition, imagery, and creativity—it is clearly a right-brain task. It requires only a personal choice, a decision to enter the path—and a mind-set receptive to what that journey might bring. At its most basic level, the labyrinth is an ancient metaphor representing a journey toward our personal, deep-est center and then back out into the world—we hope, with a broadened understanding of the journey and of the self.

During the Middles Ages, labyrinth designs in various forms were often found in Gothic cathedrals. Perhaps the most famous ancient labyrinth is the one in the nave of

Chartres Cathedral, about sixty miles southwest of Paris. Built around 1200, the Chartres labyrinth consists of four meandering quadrants that lead to the center. At the center of the floor design, there is a rosette, a medieval symbol of enlightenment. In the Middle Ages, the labyrinth was used "as a pilgrimage and/or for repentance. As a pilgrimage it was a questing, searching journey with the hope of becoming closer to God. When used for repentance the pilgrims would walk on their knees. Sometimes this eleven-circuit labyrinth would serve as a substitute for an actual pilgrimage to Jerusalem and as a result came to be called the 'Chemin de Jerusalem' or Road to Jerusalem" (see the Chartres labyrinth online at: http://www.lessons4living.com/chartres_labyrinth.htm).

One of my most powerful labyrinth experiences took place a few years ago during a weeklong silent retreat at Cedarbrake Renewal Center in Belton, Texas. Modeled after the Chartres labyrinth design, the outdoor labyrinth at Cedarbrake is particularly unusual in that it includes the trees originally present on that piece of land, making them part of the labyrinth experience. As pilgrims walk this particular labyrinth, they may need to duck down in order not to hit their heads on a tree branch—or they may have to bend around a low limb so as to remain on the path and on the way to the center. As a culmination of our retreat, Pat, our director, suggested on the last night that the whole group walk the labyrinth at the same time. Although during the week I had walked the labyrinth at the same time as some of the other retreatants, I couldn't imagine so many of us meandering through this labyrinth together. What resulted, however, was a beautiful and powerful union of hearts and feet and love as we all instinctively waited in a crowded center for the last person to arrive, before anyone stepped out to walk back into the world. Once everyone was at the center, we silently and spontaneously held hands and offered prayers of thanksgiving, and then someone's beautiful voice led us in singing "Amazing Grace."

Whether indoors or outdoors, walking a labyrinth serves as a centering tool for me. When I am tired of walking this life journey and I feel the way is too long, it reminds me that there is only *one* path I must follow, the path to the one who is my center. I've discovered that if life seems like too much work, that may be because I am approaching my pilgrimage as a maze or a puzzle to be solved rather than as the one path to which God has called me. I may have to duck down and miss the tree branch, but my task is simply to stay on the path. I breathe in the Spirit as I walk and allow the way of the labyrinth to take me home to the one who is my life and my love. The only choice I must make is whether or not to walk. This, too, is a metaphor for Christ's call to discipleship. Will I begin or continue the journey? Will I choose to stay on the path? Will I let him lead me home?

Walking with Scripture

The anonymous author and main character of the spiritual classic *The Way of a Pilgrim* is a simple Russian peasant who refers to himself as the "Pilgrim." From the opening page of the story, we learn that the Pilgrim sets out on a quest to understand how to live the meaning of Paul's first letter to the Thessalonians, specifically, the instruction to "[p]ray without ceasing" (5:17). Moved by his earnest longing for uninterrupted communion with God, the Pilgrim searches for a person to explain this mystery to him. "Please explain to me how the mind can be always set on God, not to be distracted but continuously praying" (Helen Bacovcin, p. 15), the Pilgrim asks one spiritual master after another. "How is it possible to pray continuously? I am very eager to know this and cannot in any way comprehend it" (p. 14). Like many of us, the Pilgrim in this story hoped and desired to make God the center of his life, no matter what his daily circumstances. Life was quite hard on the Pilgrim, who had lost both his material possessions and his family. He had no home, and a handicap prevented him from earning a living; so he wandered from one place to the next.

But the Pilgrim was deeply in love with God and never tired of communicating with him. And God heard the desires of his heart and led him to a monastery elder who taught him a prayer exercise that would help him achieve "the ceaseless activity of the heart" (p. 21). The elder instructed the Pilgrim to recite the name of Jesus vocally, as often as possible, throughout the day by repeating the words, "Lord Jesus Christ, have mercy on me!" (p. 21). As this prayer became a true habit of the heart, the Pilgrim learned to set aside his mind and thoughts and to focus on the Holy Spirit dwelling within him. Every breath, every step he took in his daily pilgrimage, took him closer to the awareness that God lived within him. The gem of the Pilgrim's story is its simple and honest presentation of the power of prayer, a gift available to all who thirst and hunger for God.

Much as the Pilgrim did in this nineteenth-century story, we, too, can walk with a sacred phrase or passage of Scripture. Whether we are doing a physical activity with a rhythmic action—such as walking or jogging—or simply going through our day-to-day activities, we can, literally, allow the words of Scripture to be in sync with our breath through repetition. The following are just a few examples of Scripture passages you might use: "I have the strength for everything through him who empowers me" (Phil 4:13). "The LORD is my shepherd; there is nothing I lack" (Ps 23:1). "My grace is sufficient for you" (2 Cor 12:9). "Give thanks to the Lord, for he is good, for his mercy endures forever" (Dn 3:89). "I am the resurrection and the life; whoever believes in me, even if he dies, will live" (Jn 11:25).

Walking with Scripture is a practice I learned from my longtime friend Pat, who explains it this way: "You become what you think, and to meditate on a piece of Scripture that has touched your heart is very powerful." For Pat, it is as certain as it is evident that she never walks alone, either literally or spiritually. Whether on her daily walk around the neighborhood or walking her way through a long pilgrimage, Pat reminds me, a host of people eternally walk with her—and with me. There is such grace in trusting the company of the communion of saints, including the legion of friends who "cheer" us on our spiritual journey, as Pat says, and who are always present in our hearts and on our daily walk.

In the summer of 2003, Pat and I made a major, once-in-a-lifetime pilgrimage together. For thirty-five days, we walked approximately three hundred miles of El Camino de Santiago, the ancient pilgrimate route across northern Spain. Beginning in Pamplona, Pat and I united ourselves to legions of pilgrims across time and from around the world as we walked west to the city of Santiago de Compostela, named after the apostle St. James, in northwestern Spain.

Even though this pilgrimage is one that Pat and I had talked about doing together for several years, when we first set the dates and confirmed our plans, I was paralyzed by a long list of fears. How could I possibly do such a pilgrimage? What was I thinking when I agreed to do this with Pat? What made me think that I, of all people, could walk five hundred miles across the north of Spain? Frankly, I was thankful to hear that Pat, too, shared in this initial stage of shock and fear. The reality is that the angels of darkness will always remain diligent in their work to steer us away from the Light. Yet our task is to remain faithful in prayer and to call this what it is—a temptation to step away from our pilgrim path. And while the temptations and the fears are a natural and real part of our journey, we are called to remember that light and love will always be stronger than darkness. Walking with Scripture, remembering the prayers and the Scriptures that have touched our hearts, is a wonderful way to be reminded of this truth. As Pat says, "God responds to our slightest step. We just have to give him room to work."

Living in the Present

Michael and I joke that our Siberian husky, Lobo (who truly does look like a wolf, as his Spanish name implies), has a gift for teaching us deep lessons about living in the present moment. Sometimes in the light of the afternoon, Lobo will stand perfectly still in the backyard and raise his nose into the air, smelling the scents present there. In the snow, he will dig his nose into the white stuff or even roll in it with delight, as if wanting to feel it as well as see and walk on it. And as we walk through the neighborhood on our evening walks, Lobo will often suddenly stop to look up, as if something important just crossed his path and is now in the trees. I don't know what he's looking at or smelling in the air, but when I see Lobo, I, too, take a big breath into my lungs and make a point of looking up—at the trees, at the birds flying above me, at the stars shining over us. In a very real way, Lobo reminds me of the most important spiritual practice of all, waking up to the presence of God in every moment of my day.

In his book *The Mindful Traveler*, Jim Currie describes the Buddhist practice of mindfulness, or attentiveness, as an invitation to pause and take in the marvel of the moment:

> The Buddha taught that on everyone's path are a series of opportunities, hindrances, and obstacles that in some way reflect what is inside us. Inner and outer reality dance together, giving us a chance to affirm our own higher powers and break out of our conditioned responses, attachments, and self-limitations. In some cases this simply requires breathing deeply and letting anxieties pass. In other cases, it requires taking stock of our surroundings, penetrating self-created distortions, asking ourselves—what is the big picture here? What is the pattern that I am caught up in? What choices am I making that determine my day? What forces and energies are at work that I am pointlessly opposing? (p. 4)

Every day, we are engaged in a miracle, wrote Vietnamese monk Thich Nhat Hanh. This is a miracle "which we don't even recognize: a blue sky, white clouds, green leaves, the black, curious eyes of a child—our own two eyes. All is a miracle. . . . [M]indfulness itself is the life of awareness: the presence of mindfulness means the presence of life, and therefore mindfulness is also the fruit. Mindfulness frees us of forgetfulness and dispersion and makes it possible to live fully each minute of life. Mindfulness enables us to live" (pp. 12–15). All you have to do, he said, is "[l]ive the actual moment. Only this actual moment is life. Don't be attached to the future. Don't worry about things you have to do. Don't think about getting up or taking off to do anything. Don't think about 'departing.' . . . Whatever you do, do it in mindfulness" (p. 30).

In our Catholic tradition, living in the present moment is at the heart of living in the Spirit, of knowing that God is—and that he lives—in the here and now. Saints, mystics, and contemplatives throughout the centuries have written about the importance of recognizing the presence of God in each moment. In the brief yet powerful work *Abandonment to Divine Providence*, the eighteenth-century French mystic and Jesuit priest Jean-Pierre de Caussade challenged believers to embrace the present moment as an ever-flowing source of holiness. He explained it this way:

> Every moment we live through is like an ambassador who declares the will of God. . . . Everything works to this end and, without exception, helps us toward holiness. We can find all that is necessary in the present moment. We need not worry about whether to pray or be silent, whether to withdraw into retreat or mix with people, to read or write. . . . What does matter is what each moment produces by the will of God. We must strip ourselves naked . . . so that we can be wholly submissive to God's will and so delight him. Our only satisfaction must be to live in the present moment as if there were nothing to expect beyond it. (pp. 50–51).

Whenever we are worried or distracted and we find it difficult to stay in the present, we can focus on our breathing. The

Hebrew word for "spirit" used in the Bible, *ruah*, also means "breath," reminding us in more than a symbolic way that every breath we take is God's gift of presence, his spirit within us. As we grow in our spiritual walk, we are invited to let go of the past and stop thinking about the future, and instead to trust that God's providence has already foreseen what we need in *this* moment. As the poster in our bathroom reminds me daily, when I live in the mistakes and regrets of the past, life is hard. God is not there. His name is not "I was." When I live in the problems and fears of the future, it is hard. God is not there. His name is not "I will be." When I live in the here and the now, in this moment, it is not hard. God is here. Be still, says God, and know that *I am* God (Ps 46:11).

As is often true of what is most important, this simple truth is much harder to live by than it sounds. If I adopt this view of life, I assume that I already have the grace to live each moment of the day. This theology of abundance is central to Christianity. After all, every time I pray the Our Father, I am asking God for the grace to accept and to welcome what *he* decides is my "daily bread"—which means that I trust God to provide me with all that I truly need, every step, every minute, every hour of my day.

To live in the present is to live each day as a new and unknown beginning, a gift from a God who loves us and who desires to bring us closer to him as we journey home. Living in the present enables me to see blessing in every aspect of my day, in every moment and every situation. It helps me remember that no matter what messages the prince of darkness sends my way, I belong to God and God will not only give me all I need but also make me all I need to be. To live in the moment is to be aware, to wake up, to be mindful enough to see and to hear, and to face every moment with eyes, ears, and heart open.

"Imagine that we could live each day as a day full of promises. Imagine that we could walk through the new year always listening to a voice saying to us: 'I have a gift for you and can't wait for you to see it!'" wrote Catholic author Henri Nouwen (*Here and Now*, p. 16). As Nouwen explained:

> It's hard to live in the present. The past and the future keep harassing us. The past with guilt, the future with worries. So many things have happened in our lives about which we feel uneasy, regretful, angry, confused, or at least, ambivalent. . . . These "oughts" keep us feeling guilty about the past and prevent us from being fully present to the moment. Worse, however, than our guilt are our worries. . . . These many "ifs" can so fill our mind that we become blind to the flowers in the garden and the smiling children on the streets, or deaf to the grateful voice of a friend. . . . But real life takes place in the here and now. God is a God of the present. God is always in the moment, be that moment hard or easy, joyful or painful. . . . That's why Jesus came to wipe away the burden of the past and the worries of the future. He wants us to discover God right where we are, here and now. (*Here and Now*, pp. 17–18)

How do we live fully awake and mindful of each moment? By becoming prayerful pilgrims. It is in prayer that we meet, in a personal and intimate way, the God who loves us. No matter what form our daily prayer takes—reading the Scripture, meditating on the life or the writings of a saint, saying the rosary—it is important that we also include as part of our prayer a time for silence, a time to learn to listen.

How long we pray is not as important as being faithful to the discipline of daily prayer. Whether we go to silent prayer for ten, twenty, or thirty minutes every day, it is in that time that we begin to see that there exists a space deep in our center where God *already* dwells. And it is in that holy, precious space in our hearts that we will be made whole and holy. We will be re-created in the image of our loving Creator.

I can't overemphasize the importance of committing to daily prayer—and of including silence as part of our prayer time. I am often restless, ready to get busy with daily living again. Yet what is important is that I am faithful to the discipline. I say to God that I am here, that I am open to whatever graces he has in mind for me right now. And then I stop talking, and I listen. I open my heart and submit my will to his hand in my life. This is the most important part of my day and, truly, of my Christian pilgrimage.

Learning to be attentive to God's moment-by-moment presence is one of the most helpful disciplines for the person who is on a journey, whether the travel is interior or on a road in a distant place. With each step, we can learn that we are loved and that God's grace surrounds us.

Our Compass Home

Long before I could grapple with the theology of transubstantiation—or even try to pronounce that word!—the Eucharist had a special meaning to me. My heart understood that the Eucharist was a unique gift that Jesus Christ left for us, a way for every Christian to get to know him intimately. I have somehow always known that this type of food could nourish something in me that even now I struggle to name. The Eucharist also reminds me that I belong. In a real, if mystical, way, the eucharistic celebration heals and answers our inner need of belonging. "I have called you by name. You are mine!" says the Lord. And in Christ, we are, literally, one with him and with one another.

Perhaps as pilgrims on our journey home, there is no greater compass than the Eucharist. And I do want it and hunger for it every day. As I struggled with nowhere to call home while growing up, it was being Catholic—being claimed by something bigger than myself—and the communion I felt with Christ and his people in the Eucharist that gave me a much-needed security. In a daily life of new houses and new schools that felt eternally unfamiliar, I could count on being one with something and someone else. When everything else in my life was transitory, I was nevertheless at home on Sunday mornings.

Even though the parish we attended changed frequently because we often visited assorted parishes where my parents' priest friends from Cuba were assigned, it didn't matter. It was at Mass that I could claim to belong, even when no one there knew me. This was the one place, regardless of the particular church we attended, where I "fit." Together, we stood and professed our faith as believers in one and the same God, and we received in the Eucharist the gift of Christ's presence right here and now. Even when I couldn't understand these abstract concepts, I knew on a more intuitive level that the community of faith that claimed me became one Body in our one Lord, Jesus Christ. My heart understood what I even now struggle to explain in words.

This truth has never abandoned me. In the Jubilee Year 2000, as my husband and I and our four children traveled throughout Europe together, we began our pilgrimage in every city by visiting the local cathedral or church and praying together there. Most of the time, our prayer was as simple as walking up to the altar, kneeling together, and holding hands in a circle as we said a Hail Mary or the Our Father.

During those two and a half months of travel, we often stumbled upon a Mass about to start, so we'd stay. We celebrated Mass in many languages—Italian, German, French, Dutch, and Spanish. I do wish I had been able to understand what was being said, especially during the homily. But I can honestly say that, for me, celebrating Mass with the local community was a way of experiencing church unlike any I had ever encountered before. Or perhaps it is more accurate to say that celebrating Mass in different languages expanded my understanding of that mystical body of believers that I had already experienced as a child.

We belong to a *catholic* church—literally, a universal community. In practical terms, this meant that by using our Sunday missals, we knew what readings were being read whether or not we understood the language in Assisi or Salzburg. And the parts of the Mass, the flow of the eucharistic celebration, was always consistent, even with each country's unique nuances. Nothing can describe the solidarity created when a diverse group of people joins together in receiving the body of Christ. It strengthened my pilgrim heart to know that no matter where I was, I was still part of that community of faith in a mystical but authentic sense. I belonged. I stood with, and received Eucharist with, my brothers and sisters in faith—and this bond was much stronger than a common language, race, or ethnicity.

The Eucharist is important in another sense as well. It really is food for our journey. Not only does sharing the Eucharist unite me to my brothers and sisters, but it also nourishes and strengthens my spirit as an individual. In the bread and the wine, Jesus comes to be with me, to heal my heart and my wounded spirit. When I open myself to Christ as I am, I acknowledge humbly with the rest of the community right before communion, "Lord, I am not worthy to receive you. But only say the word, and I shall be healed." Then as I walk up to receive the eucharistic bread, I am asked to personally profess my faith and to accept the invitation. "This is the body of Christ," the priest or minister of communion says. To which I reply from the depths of my heart, "Amen!" Yes, let it be so. I believe; please help my unbelief. Come into my heart, Jesus, and heal me. Give me what I need. I trust you to be my daily bread, every day.

I can take advantage of the grace available to me in the other sacraments by regularly celebrating Mass and receiving Eucharist, by going to reconciliation, and by accepting the anointing of the sick when it is available. By choosing to have a thankful heart, I recognize the abundance that God has placed in my life and acknowledge the many ways that God provides me with my daily bread—my health, the people in my life, the sunshine and the stars, the way the leaves seem to rain down on our front yard in autumn, even the way our dog rejoices in nature.

This list of tools for the pilgrim's journey is not comprehensive but, rather, a sampling of some of the instruments that we have found helpful, both in our personal journeys and in our family's travels. As we continue learning how to walk through life *intentionally* and *attentively*, we will discover help in remarkable and unexpected forms. That, too, is one of the joys of the journey!

7

Making All Travel Sacred

~ MICHAEL ~

The thick vegetation crept ever closer as we rambled down a dirt and gravel road in a rented Toyota 4Runner. As we slowly distanced ourselves from the main road, I informed the kids that we were nearing our destination: a tropical rain forest. Michelle, who was six years old at the time, asked, "Where? I don't see it." It never occurred to me that she was expecting a glassed-in building like the "rain forests" she had encountered in Oklahoma City and Galveston, Texas. With low clouds and a forest canopy providing a roof, we spent the afternoon exploring this tropical paradise. During a break in our hike, we came to understand where the sloth got its name, by watching one navigate a tree.

We were in Costa Rica to attend the wedding of my sister, Angela, to Elliott, a native of Costa Rica. María and I celebrated our thirteenth wedding anniversary as we traveled there with our four young children and my

grandmother. In addition to a wedding and the rain forest, we experienced the strong undertow of a Costa Rican
Pacific coast surf, saw both the Atlantic and Pacific
Oceans from one spot high on a simmering volcanic
mountain, survived an earthquake, received a personal
tour of a coffee plantation, prayed at the basilica in
Cartago, and spent a memorable New Year's Eve dancing
and celebrating with locals. Our trip to Costa Rica might
have seemed like a typical family vacation, and in many
ways, it mirrored one. Most of the activities on our trip
were indistinguishable from those of the typical tourist.
On this trip, however, the difference was mostly one of
attitude and approach to travel.

María and I desire to live every day aware of our earthly
journey. With the inevitable distractions and anxieties of
daily life, we sometimes forget that we are on our own
road to greater communion with God. To heighten our
memory and deepen our response to God's call, we have at
times consciously left our home to journey as pilgrims to a
holy site. But what about all the other travel involved in
our year? Even when traveling on a summer vacation, we
should ask ourselves whether we are tourists or pilgrims. Is
the fun, relaxation, or challenge that we will find at Disney
World, on the beach, or during the backpacking trek in the
Rockies an end in itself, or is it mysteriously tied to our
life's larger purposes and journey?

We propose that all travel, precisely because it disturbs
our daily routines, presents great opportunities for height-
ened awareness of God and his universe. In other words,
even travel to the dullest business meeting can be transformed into a sacred moment. Approaching business
or pleasure travel with a pilgrim heart will enrich the
experience while reinforcing the daily journey. A tourist

consumes the travel experience—ingesting, digesting, expelling the waste, and retaining a few snapshots in the mind. The pilgrim, in contrast, absorbs the experience, attuned to the people, culture, food, and geography of the place. Like Mary, the pilgrim keeps all these things, reflecting on them in his heart (Lk 2:19). By intentionally making the business trip or family vacation sacred, the traveler also reinforces the spiritual discipline that is working to transform the 86,400 seconds of each and every ordinary day into one long canticle of praise.

How to Prepare for a Family Pilgrimage

Planning for our summer of 2000 Jubilee Year pilgrimage began in the fall of 1999. After setting the dates, we bought a map of Europe and put it up in the living room. Rome, Spain (to visit María's cousins), and Oxford were the anchors for the trip. During weekly family meetings, we began to dream about where else we might go in Europe. Finally, we asked the children to name their top destinations and share with the family why they chose those particular places. Christopher, who chose Patrick as his confirmation name and who now attends the University of Notre Dame, wanted to go, unsurprisingly, to Ireland. Anamaría chose Poitiers because of the Romanesque church she had read about in French class. Rebekah has long loved Monet's impressionist paintings and wanted to go to Giverny to see his famous gardens. We were able to accommodate all these desires. Poor Michelle, our youngest, wanted to go to Denmark and St. Petersburg because of books she had been reading. With map in hand, I showed her that both of these places were far removed from anywhere else we might travel.

From these family meetings, an itinerary slowly emerged. Assisi, Siena, and Florence were desirable destinations for us in Italy. María also wanted to take the kids to Salzburg, where she had attended a seminar a few years before. We were meeting friends in Paris, but we also wanted to travel to Lourdes. In writing *Edith Stein: St. Teresa Benedicta of the Cross*, María had connected with people in Cologne and Ghent. And, if possible, I wanted to return to the small town in Holland where I had spent my fifth-grade year. We realized early in the planning process that we needed to avoid a dizzying pace that would leave all of us exhausted and grumpy. So we were on the lookout for opportunities to intersperse museum and big-city days with more relaxing times in rural settings to refresh our spirits and our bodies.

At this point, the family gave me the jigsaw puzzle and asked me to make all the pieces fit together. I stared at the map daily for about a week, trying to envision the best way to connect all the dots.

María and I had to decide early between car and rail travel because the suitable forms of luggage would be our Christmas presents to the kids that year. All our destinations were on rail lines except my old home in rural Holland. We were also traveling through some mountainous regions, and train travel would be more relaxing for those of us who would otherwise have to drive a rental car. An added bonus of train travel would be the lack of potty stops. After doing a quick comparison of the estimated costs of each form of transportation (this is not as easy as it may sound because there are multiple rail and car rental options), we concluded that train travel would cost the same as or less than the alternative.

With our mode of transportation set, María and I looked into luggage for the kids. Although our initial thought was to get suitcases on rollers, we were advised by friends that backpacks would make it easier to get on and off trains and buses. (And I could just picture María sitting in a plaza in Siena, refusing to move because a wheel had broken off her suitcase.) We found backpacks that had zip-off day-packs attached and bought one for each of the kids.

At this point, and for the next few months, several parts of planning occurred simultaneously. In addition to a plane ticket and luggage, Santa brought each of the children a guidebook from a different country. The children then researched what we ought to see and do in that particular country and reported back to the family. As a family, we used Rick Steves's book *Europe through the Back Door*. By reading this book and talking with friends, we developed a plan for alternating between big cities and rural settings. We decided to stay in Siena and day-trip by bus to Florence, combining the must-see Renaissance art of the faster-paced Florence with the enchanting feel of evening strolls through medieval Siena. We also settled on pastoral settings along the Italian coast and in the Swiss Alps that would allow us to rest after the rigors of touring big cities.

María and I worked on different aspects of the nitty-gritty details. As María looked into lodging, it became apparent that we could stay (fairly inexpensively) in monasteries during most of the trip, which allowed us to remain closer to the pilgrim ideal of our journey. Eileen Barish's guide *Lodging in Italy's Monasteries* was invaluable in selecting the places where we would stay in Italy. Secular guidebooks and the Internet allowed us to fill the gaps in lodging.

The Internet also proved invaluable in helping us understand the European rail system. I worried that language barriers would prevent us from communicating adequately about train schedules. Knowing the rail options ahead of time—how long it takes to get from point A to point B on an express train or on the slower trains, the frequency of rail service, the types of amenities on each type of train, and whether seat reservations were required—calmed those fears. For each leg of the journey, I printed and carried with us the train schedules corresponding roughly to the time we wanted to leave a particular town.

As the trip approached, each of us was deciding what to pack, and, as a family, we were deciding what items could be shared by all. Michelle, our youngest and most organized, read a book and explored the Internet to get tips for packing for this type of trip. She then gave the family a seminar on how and what to pack.

As you can see from our planning, it would have been a lot easier to simply sign up with one of the many organized pilgrimage tours where all the arrangements are made for you. María and I have been on these types of pilgrimages and have enjoyed them immensely. For this particular trip, four factors persuaded us to strike out on our own. First, we believed that an organized tour of this length for all six of us would be cost prohibitive. Second, although the children were getting older, we thought that an organized tour with the need to keep to a preplanned schedule and agenda might be too confining. Third, we wanted to experience the tastes, sounds, and textures of the local culture as much as we possibly could, which meant strolling the plazas as we looked for places to eat and riding the city buses rather than the tour bus. Finally, the planning itself became a family pilgrimage as we worked together for months toward this common goal. I even got the children involved in drafting the budget so that as we ate our way through Europe, they understood that food was the biggest variable that could bust the budget if we weren't careful.

We probably won't ever take a trip more complex than our Jubilee Year pilgrimage. We offer the details of it to you in the hope that it might help you plan a family pilgrimage of your own. We also hope that it has sparked your imagination as to how to involve the whole family in the planning process. And we hope it offers encouragement; however expansive your pilgrimage plans are, if we could do it, so can you.

How Nature Enhances the Pilgrim's Journey

Our family likes to camp. Even a weekend away at a state park can do wonders for the soul—provided the weather cooperates. And, for a growing family on a tight budget, camping has provided an excellent way to extend vacations to places like Yellowstone and Rocky Mountain National Park. For two or three years, while the kids were young, we would camp twice a year with our small faith community. At most, we probably had ten couples with a total of thirty children under age six on a given weekend. In those days, camping was not quiet, but oddly enough, it was relaxing. Little about the weekend was overtly religious, but all of it opened us to the transcendent. Yes, we prayed before meals and sang songs like "Our God Reigns" during a prayer service. Mostly, we hiked, swam, fished, and roamed the forests and fields together. We often ate better than at home, with Dutch oven pot roast and peach cobbler for dinner and breakfast tacos in the morning. Lessons in community living were silently transmitted as the children participated in the cooking and cleaning. Scrapes were cleaned and tears were dried by any available adult. And the evenings were spent in story as the s'mores were prepared near the campfire.

Spring camping in Oklahoma or Texas can be heaven on earth, with cool, clear air bringing out the richness of the bluebonnets, Indian paintbrush, and other wildflowers dotting the landscape. Or, given the volatility of the weather, it can be a foretaste of the less-desirable eternal destination. Nature's god has sometimes answered our joyful noise with wind, rain, hail, and even an occasional tornado. I vividly remember one March evening sitting at the picnic table underneath the tarp. The map was spread out on the table, and the radio was on as we plotted the course of the tornadoes near us. Our vulnerability in the open, coupled with our contingency planning, opened us to the transcendent in a radically different way than had the nature hike that afternoon. A year later, we ended up camping at the Marriott's Residence Inn in Fort Worth, after hail and tornadoes bombarded us on the way to the campsite. We have finally learned our lesson. Last year, we looked at the weather *before* leaving home. With the possibility of severe weather hovering around 60 percent, we booked an inexpensive room for Friday night through Priceline.com, spent a pleasant evening at the hotel as the storm raged around us, and headed to the campsite refreshed on a gorgeous Saturday morning.

We have also taken longer camping trips to national parks. In the summer of 1996, after visiting my dad and his wife in De Kalb, Illinois, we met up with friends in Sioux City, Iowa. Our two families traveled together to Yellowstone, stopping at the Corn Palace, Custer State Park, Badlands National Park, Crazy Horse, and Mount Rushmore on the way. Traveling with another family meant finding a common rhythm for the journey. How often would we stop to eat? Was eating in the car allowed? How often would we change drivers? And how long would the dads make the kids wait before stopping for a potty break? Each family had done a fair amount of traveling and had established patterns for driving, setting up camp, cooking, hiking, and sightseeing. For the most part, we blended the families easily, with tensions flaring most often in tired or hungry moments.

Early one morning in Yellowstone, while our children slept, María and I prepared to drive to Hayden Valley to watch the wildlife at dawn. As she broke the thin layer of ice that had formed in our coffee pot, I grabbed the back-packing stove, coffee, filters, and two cups. In my semi-conscious state, I remembered the words of Psalm 57: "Awake, my soul; awake, lyre and harp! I will wake the dawn" (Ps 57:9). As the world awoke that crisp July morning, fog danced along the calm water, playing among the trees on the opposite shore. A fox sauntered within a few feet of us as the bison roamed in the distance. Deer, elk, moose, wolves, ospreys, trumpeter swans, sandhill cranes, and bald eagles all shared our environment. Our daughter Michelle came face to face with a black bear one afternoon. And, fortunately for all of us, the mama grizzly we saw with her three cubs was a great distance away.

Belching, passing gas, and spitting are considered rude behaviors, at least when engaged in by humans. In Yellowstone, these activities are oddly attractive when dredged up from the bowels of the earth. In this oldest and largest national park, the earth itself literally breathes, bringing Paul's words to life: "all creation is groaning in labor pains even until now" (Rom 8:22). The geysers spew their liquid heavenward like a child playing at the pool on a summer afternoon. Hot springs mesmerize onlookers with an alluring array of blues, yellows, greens, oranges, and purples created by minerals, algae, and bacteria. Fumaroles—volcanic openings spewing gas and smoke—abound, as do mud pots. The distinct smell of sulfur lingers in the summer air. Decaying bison remains can be found near some hot springs where, in an ill-fated attempt to stay warm the previous winter, a bison wandered too close to one of these thermal wonders.

Yellowstone's ten-thousand-foot Mount Washburn provided us with a wonderful hiking experience. The day started with a little tension because our friend John and I each had our own ideas about how best to pack our lunch, snacks, and backpacking stove. After ironing out this minor wrinkle, we set out at a fairly leisurely pace. As we made our ascent, we walked through what had once been a densely covered forest. After the fires of 1988, all that remained of this old forest were the scarred and barren trunks of lodgepole pines dozens of feet high, haphazardly dotting the landscape as if they had been giant match-sticks stuck in the ground. In the midst of the devastation, new growth emerged: rich grasses and sapling lodgepoles three or four feet high. A National Park Service brochure, which could have been written about our own pilgrim journey, explains that "without the cleansing, culling, and regenerative contributions of fire, a dynamic ecosystem becomes a stagnant garden, piling up dead fuels and choking on its own debris." In a remarkable parallel to the spiritual life, the brochure adds, "Only the most arid deserts can maintain diversity without the aid of fire." Upon reaching the top of Mount Washburn, we had a glorious view of the park. We spotted snow-covered peaks jutting out of the clouds ninety miles to the south and understood how Grand Teton and the other major mountains in the Teton range got their name from French fur trappers nearly two hundred years ago.

For me, spending time in nature brings to life Hana-niah, Azariah, and Mishael's song of praise from inside the fiery furnace:

Bless the Lord, all you works of the Lord.
Praise and exalt him above all forever. . . .
Sun and moon, bless the Lord.
Stars of heaven, bless the Lord.
Every shower and dew, bless the Lord.
All you winds, bless the Lord.
Fire and heat, bless the Lord.
Cold and chill, bless the Lord.
Dew and rain, bless the Lord.
Frost and chill, bless the Lord.
Ice and snow, bless the Lord.
Nights and days, bless the Lord.
Light and darkness, bless the Lord.
Lightnings and clouds, bless the Lord.
Let the earth bless the Lord.
Praise and exalt him above all forever.
Mountains and hills, bless the Lord.
Everything growing from the earth, bless the Lord.
You springs, bless the Lord.
Seas and rivers, bless the Lord.
You dolphins and water creatures, bless the Lord.
All you birds of the air, bless the Lord.
All you beasts of the air, bless the Lord.
You sons of men, bless the Lord.

Dn 3:57–88, Liturgy of the Hours

Nature enhances the pilgrim's journey simply by being there. Our part is to take the time to witness nature. María and I try to do this regularly, and we have made countless opportunities for our children to do the same. When standing before a natural wonder of the world, no sermons or lessons are necessary; God's creation speaks very eloquently for itself.

I love to watch our Siberian husky, Lobo, as I let him out in the morning. After taking a few steps into the backyard, he raises his snout skyward and leisurely drinks in the morning air.

We are so easily distracted by our work and schedules and possessions that we rarely listen well to what the wind and trees, rivers and mountains are saying. Thus a journey outdoors can be a valuable pilgrimage, and it's not difficult to get to nature. We can camp for a week in a national park, or we can spend a few moments mere steps from the back door, heads lifted like Lobo.

How Family Vacations Can Become Blessed Events

On a pleasant Monday afternoon in August of 2002, María and I, along with our four children, drove from my dad's house in Charlottesville through the northern Virginia countryside, with the Blue Ridge Mountains accompanying us to the west, into Washington, D.C., past the Capitol, and toward Catholic University. We parked and walked up the hill toward the Basilica of the National Shrine of the Immaculate Conception. My children, who had been to the great cathedrals of Europe, were awestruck by the grandeur of "America's Catholic church," which they hadn't seen since the last time we visited Washington, D.C., several years before. Touring Monticello and walking the grounds of the University of Virginia during the previous week, we had pondered America's commitment to religious liberty. Now, as we walked through the massive structure toward the Crypt

Church, the mosaic of our faith unfolded before our eyes as we viewed the multiple side chapels dedicated to Mary by various immigrant groups. In this place, *E pluribus unum*—one out of many—became a vibrant reality.

This would be the last time the six of us would be together until Christmas. In the crypt church, we received the sacrament of reconciliation. After Mass, we drove the short distance to the suburban Maryland house of one of our son's college buddies. From there, Christopher and his friend would head to Cleveland and more friends. Then Christopher would go by bus to Wisconsin and another friend before finally arriving in St. Paul, Minnesota, where he would spend five weeks training for his year as a member of NET Ministries, during which he would travel the country, giving retreats for high school and junior high students. The rest of us would spend a couple of days in D.C. and then head for the beach. The shrine had been an indispensable part of our day as we came together in prayer, María and I once again commending our children to God's loving care as one of them prepared to leave us.

The family is the primary school, teaching the art of communal living to children (and adults). But the pace of our lives puts this school to the test weekly. A typical February week in the Scaperlanda house, for example, includes Mass (we aim for three or four times a week), four nights of basketball games, a debate and acting tournament, confirmation classes, youth group, and piano. Add to that a church meeting or booster-club meeting, and you get the picture. The children have homework and want to spend time with their friends. In the midst of what can only be described as semiorganized chaos, we do everything possible to eat dinner together daily, pray together in the evening, and attend Mass together on Sunday. To accomplish this, we might eat at 4:30 one afternoon and 9:30 the next night.

Family vacations give us the chance to leave the hectic pace behind and spend time with one another in a more leisurely setting. God doesn't stay behind in Norman, Oklahoma, when the Scaperlanda family hits the road. In a formal way, we continue to remind ourselves that God is at the center of our lives. We start our trips with an Our Father, a Hail Mary, and a Glory Be. We pray Night Prayer from the Liturgy of the Hours together, as we do at home. And we go to Mass on Sundays and sometimes during the week. Mass away from home can be a fun adventure as we celebrate our unity in the midst of diversity. At St. Andrew by the Sea Parish on North Padre Island, most of the parishioners around us were clad in shorts on a rainy Sunday morning; their permanent church structure had no walls, which allowed the salty air and the sound of seagulls to fill the sanctuary. At St. Stephen's Cathedral in Vienna, Austria, we were pleasantly surprised to see a large number of people, many clearly on their way home from work, attending weekday Mass in the heart of what is rapidly becoming secular Europe.

Arriving in Oxford after three weeks of traveling the Continent, we looked forward to attending Mass in English. Our first Sunday there, we chose the 11 A.M. Mass at St. Aloysius, just down Woodstock Road from our house. Cardinal Newman had been instrumental in founding this oratory, and it had been the home parish of J. R. R. Tolkien. We arrived a little late and found a packed church with a good mix of couples and their children, the elderly, and university students. The other masses at

St. Aloysius, were in English, but this Mass, to our surprise and my delight, was in Latin. A further surprise awaited us after Mass. Instead of coffee and doughnuts in the church hall, I drank a pint of ale at the church's social club.

Although prayer and Mass remind us of God's presence as we travel, most manifestations of God's presence are more informal. Most of our trips are by van, where we can spend anywhere from four to fourteen hours together in a day. Living in such close proximity requires great patience and honing the art of compromise as seats are allocated and movies chosen. When the kids were young, María and I would fight over who got to drive because driving was easier than changing diapers and cleaning up after crying babies. Now I have to wrestle the children for the steering wheel as we hit the open road.

Train travel in Europe provided very different opportunities for togetherness. On the emptier trains, we often spread out, each taking his or her own compartment in order to sleep or read uninterrupted. But we came together as a unit to make sure we all got off the train with our belongings intact. One time, our efficiency nearly got the best of us. We were traveling from Interlaken, Switzerland, to Cologne, Germany, with a change of trains in Freiburg, Germany. We were all dozing, thinking we had plenty of time, when all of a sudden one of us was jolted out of slumber by the announcement that Freiburg was the next station. We stuffed our belongings haphazardly into backpacks and exited the train. We looked at our watches and knew it was too early to be in Freiburg. Temporarily setting aside my male aversion to asking directions or seeking help, I approached the conductor, who laughed and told us we were in Fribourg, Switzerland, not Freiburg, Germany! Our minds still groggy from sleep, we reboarded the train just as it was leaving the station.

Lingering dinners highlight the family vacation for me. With nowhere else to go and no one else to see, we have occasionally fallen into hours of conversation and laughter. The distractions of life at home make it all but impossible to duplicate this presence to one another and to the moment. After a busy day of sightseeing in Rome, we would stroll the streets and the piazzas in the late evening and soak in the ambience of this ancient city as we looked for an outdoor trattoria where we could sit and enjoy pasta or pizza while sampling the house wine. After dinner, if we hadn't had our gelato (calling it "ice cream" doesn't do it justice) for the day—and sometimes even if we had—we would find a place serving this heavenly delight, duck inside, get our order, and rejoin the crowds strolling through the city. One night, as we were walking from the Trevi Fountain (yes, we left a few coins in the water) to the Spanish Steps, I wondered out loud if anyone was at home watching television, because the whole city seemed to be out "wasting" time in friendship.

To the untrained eye, this might not seem like sacred travel: Rome, food, and wine! Can fantasies-come-true be sacred? In truth, the Italian atmosphere merely provided a nonessential backdrop, albeit an impressive one, for the sacred aspect of this travel. Christ became incarnate as we came together as a family for the pure enjoyment of one another. If only for a moment, old arguments were suspended, and new vistas in our relationships opened before us. We knew that the day would come when we would have to descend from this mountaintop experience and return to the world of school and work. We also knew that the old arguments would emerge once again as tensions mounted in the daily grind, but in these grace-filled moments, we had a taste of the kind of fellowship that is possible.

Time embraced eternity as these long evenings flowed into early mornings. The rhythm of life slowed as if we were floating lazily down a river instead of paddling furiously against the current. We built this pattern into our whole Jubilee Year trip, alternating between heavy sight-seeing agendas in big cities and more relaxed exploration in small towns or villages. Assisi followed Rome, and a small village in the Swiss Alps followed Vienna and Salzburg.

What we see on these family vacations can add to the pilgrim experience. Rome's Coliseum, the concentration camps, and the remnants of the Berlin Wall remind us of the horrors that result when human beings abuse their freedom. Several years ago, we took the children to the United States Holocaust Memorial Museum in Washington, D.C. As the Nazi atrocities unfolded before our eyes, humanity's capacity for evil presented itself in undeniable form. At the same time, we experienced glimmers of hope in the many stories of Holocaust victims who survived against all odds and of Christians who risked everything to shelter their Jewish brethren. Hope (not to be confused with romantic optimism) blossomed as I recalled St. Maximilian Kolbe's sacrifice and Viktor Frankl's descriptions, in *Man's Search for Meaning*, of heroic self-giving by prisoners who had been stripped of everything but a tattooed number. In impossible circumstances, these persons had fully lived the pilgrimage.

In contrast to the sobering experience of the Holocaust Memorial Museum, the International Spy Museum in Washington, D.C., is downright fun. It displays spy gadgets, espionage, international intrigue, wiretaps, hidden cameras, decoder devices, and feigned love. The imagination runs wild in this interactive playground.

Even this provided an opportunity for sacred travel as the complexities of the human spirit and the ingenuity of the human mind came to life. Human depravity was evident in the lives of traitorous double agents who sold out their countries for personal monetary gain. The nuances and ethical dilemmas of living in a world where the kingdom of God already exists but is not yet fully manifested were drawn out by the measures employed and compromises made to combat the forces of evil in the world.

Sometimes family trips can be so tiring that we feel as if we need a vacation from the vacation. We often want to maximize our time and our dollar by seeing as much as possible. If we are not mindful, our desire to *do* will triumph over our need to *be*. Family vacations become blessed events because we choose to make room and time for the sacred.

How to Transform Business Travel

A blanket of white covered Montreal on a subzero January night as the taxi drove me from a business dinner to St. Joseph's Oratory on Mount Royal. The previous night, I had stayed on the fourteenth floor of a Hiltonesque hotel. The room was spacious and was fitted with a color TV, three telephones (you have to have one in the bathroom), Internet access, a coffee pot, and my own iron and ironing board. If I had been short on ethics and long on luggage space, the hotel's down comforter would have come home with me. The guest room at the oratory's John XXIII Pavilion, in contrast, was simple but adequately appointed. It had none of the amenities of the hotel and no private bath. Delighted, I arrived at the oratory about fifteen minutes before the office closed at 10:00 P.M., and was tucked in my bed by 10:30.

After breakfast the next morning, I walked through the snow to the oratory itself, where I spent the day becoming acquainted with the story of Brother André, his miraculous healing powers, and his dream of building a tribute to St. Joseph. I also reflected on the life of St. Joseph. It may seem natural that I, as a father of four, would have a devotion to Jesus' foster father, but I must confess that the thought had never occurred to me. At forty-two years of age and with children fast approaching adulthood, I finally began asking St. Joseph to join his wife in praying for the protection and well-being of my children.

I find that most business trips provide prime opportunities for sacred travel. With daily routines at home and work temporarily suspended, the business traveler often passes excess time in a sports bar, a hotel lounge, watching TV in the hotel room, or reading the latest novel. I've done these things myself, and I'm not condemning anyone else who does. But any trip is an opportunity to present myself to God as a stranger in a strange land. My trip to Montreal itself grew out of a series of unexpected blessings. As a law professor and scholar, I am passionately interested in studying the connection between freedom and truth, and how the relationship between them plays out in a pluralistic society. I am also interested in exploring the role of religion in shaping the culture and informing our laws. My son, Christopher, knew of these professional interests and invited me to a conference at Notre Dame directly on point. As a result of that conference, I was invited to present a paper in November of 2002 at Baylor University. At Baylor, I had a five-minute conversation with a gentleman from Montreal named J.-Robert. It was one of those rare times when a bond instantly forms. During that short time, we discussed Thérèse of Lisieux and Mother Teresa. I later learned that he and I shared the same passions and that he had spent the last twenty years attempting to run his three profitable companies on the basis of the Catholic understanding of the transcendent dignity of each and every human person. He was putting into practice in a business setting what I was studying in the legal and cultural setting.

A week or so after returning from Baylor, I received an e-mail from J.-Robert inviting me to a conference that would explore the "conciliation of the growth of human well-being with productivity and profits." On the afternoon before the conference, J.-Robert and I spent an hour in his office talking about our families, our faith, and our pilgrimages. After our discussion, he and I adjourned to the company's "quiet" room, a small and simply adorned prayer room, where we prayed in communion with Mother Teresa, who had prayed in that same room in the 1980s. At the conference itself, one participant gave a beautiful reflection on the sacredness of work, and I made new connections between the issues facing the business community and those facing the legal community. This journey started with a phone call by a nineteen-year-old college freshman to his dad. A series of coincidences, or grace?

Normally, when I travel on business, I don't take a day to spend in prayer and reflection, as I did in Montreal, but I try to take a few extra minutes or hours to specifically remember that the trip is part of my sacred walk with and toward God. Six months after September 11, 2001, I had a meeting in D.C. that started on a Friday morning. I arrived at my Capitol Hill–area hotel room on Thursday afternoon with some time to kill before dinner. From a previous trip, I remembered that there was a Catholic church on the south or southeast side of the Capitol. After checking in, I ventured out, passing a locked-down Capitol, where police with dogs and mirrors were thoroughly checking each car as it approached a makeshift barricade. My memory took me back to my childhood, when entry into the Capitol was unobstructed by police or guard. I found the church, and it was unlocked. After my quiet time sitting before the Lord, I noticed a kneeler at a side altar before the Blessed Virgin. I knelt and prayed the rosary. In all, it added about an hour to my trip, not counting the pleasant but jarring walk past the Capitol. But it helped me put the trip in perspective, reminding me of my eternal destination.

When I travel for pleasure or business, I don't want to leave my faith at home. And if I have half a day or even half an hour that isn't controlled by someone else's agenda, I try to find a sacred place where my spiritual desire for communion with God can be fed in a physical space meant for worship. I usually find myself in Chicago, Washington, D.C., and South Bend, Indiana, at least twice a year, and I have developed sacred patterns in each of these locations. In Chicago, I make it a habit to make my confession and attend Mass at Holy Name Cathedral. If the weather isn't too bad, the walk down Michigan Avenue is an added bonus. In D.C., I follow a similar routine at the Basilica of the National Shrine of the Immaculate Conception. And at Notre Dame, I try to go directly to the grotto when I arrive, to thank Mary for her intercession.

For less familiar destinations, I often use my own background knowledge, friends, guidebooks, the Internet, and the hotel concierge. Often the diocesan Web site for the destination city will have information of interest for Catholic visitors, such as a list of churches and religious houses where you can attend Mass or pray the Liturgy of the Hours publicly.

Before any business trip, my friend Jeff always researches the area (he doesn't mind driving for two or three hours, so his idea of "area" is rather large) to find a place with some sacred meaning to explore. Several years ago while in Chicago on business, his research led the two of us to Wheaton, Illinois, where we enjoyed seeing the desk where Tolkien wrote *The Hobbit*, the wardrobe that sparked C. S. Lewis's imagination in *The Lion, the Witch, and the Wardrobe*, and Lewis's personal library. Jeff also consciously tries to add a birding or nature expedition to the end of any business trip. For him, nature itself adds a spiritual element to travel, and he has learned that it enhances his day-to-day pilgrimage.

In the end, whether taking the time to do a little research or acting spontaneously, the physical space is less important than the posture of openness toward God and his presence on the journey.

Sometimes merely asking questions can help us focus in a more spiritual way upon our daily path: What person, culture, or work of nature has been presented to me at this moment? How do I respond to this gift?

January seems to be my month for unexpected travel. During a trip to Portugal in January of 2002, I found myself sitting in the hotel bar with M. J. Akbar, a writer from India. As we talked about his forthcoming book, *The Shade of Swords: Jihad and the Conflict between Islam and Christianity*, he suggested that the biggest clash between these two civilizations was not between two differing faith traditions but, rather, between one civilization (Islam) that had retained its faith and the other civilization (the

Christian West) that had abandoned its faith. Although I suspect he realized the situation was much more complex than he had presented it, I knew he spoke much truth about the Christian, or post-Christian, West. Do we as a society live as if Christ's life, passion, death, and resurrection are the pivotal events in all of history? Do we as individuals organize our lives around this central truth of our faith? Do we live as if we understand the reality that "it is only in the mystery of the Word made flesh that the mystery" of the human person truly becomes clear (Vatican II document, "Gaudium et Spes," paragraph 22)? Like the sun trying to penetrate a dense morning fog, these questions had for some time been trying to penetrate my very dense head. It took a surprise encounter with a Muslim from India to clear away the fog.

The sacred is everywhere just waiting to be recognized by the often weary traveler. At its core, sacred travel requires an openness to the unfolding drama of our lives. It requires that attention be paid to the present. And remembering that our earthly travels are part of a much larger drama can transform even the bleakest business trip, making it a vital part of our pilgrim journey. This takes no advance planning, merely awareness of the journey, but even a little advance planning can enhance the experience.

I propose that on your next trip you take a little extra time to place yourself intentionally in God's presence. For instance, at home, I pray the morning office from the Liturgy of the Hours alone and night prayer with my family. On the road, I try to add evening prayer into the mix. At home, I take my quiet time for twenty or thirty minutes in my living room. On the road, I will often try to find a church where I can spend this time in front of the tabernacle. At home, I am horrible at journaling. On the road, I try to spend a few minutes making my illegible mark in the travel journal María bought me.

It is also important that the traveler maintain—and even increase—his daily spiritual exercises. The road is no place to abstain from Mass, the rosary, Bible reading, devotionals, or whatever form of spiritual discipline you exercise at home. Being away from home and what is familiar presents great possibilities, but it also increases the dangers. Travel, at least travel without family, can lower one's defenses and increase temptations, as the traveler finds himself alone without the usual lines of support and accountability. Maintaining and even supplementing one's spiritual diet helps counteract the temptations by presenting an open posture toward God's protecting grace.

Just as travel presents opportunities for the tempter to lead us astray, it also creates opportunities for God's infinite love to penetrate our consciousness, which is often anesthetized by the numbing daily routine. New surroundings can startle us into paying better attention in general, and the change of pace provided by travel can also allow us to experience even our usual spiritual disciplines in a fresh way.

With the rosary (which can be said anywhere, anytime, and under almost any condition, using fingers to keep track of the decades if need be) in particular, the traveler can, to use the Holy Father's words from his recent Apostolic Letter *Rosarium Virginis Mariae*, "sit at the school of Mary" and be "led to contemplate the beauty on the face of Christ and to experience the depths of his love" (Paragraph 1). Whether it is through the rosary or some other act of prayer, take extra time on the road to open yourself to God. You won't regret it.

Attitude Is Everything

The stories you have read are true, and the names have *not* been changed to protect the innocent. And I confess that our stories have a positive spin because that is generally how we approach travel. We have heard other people describe travel to some of the same places, and their accounts were quite different, focusing on all the long lines, inadequate facilities, unfriendly people, and unappetizing food.

Negative things do happen on our trips. We had a passport fiasco that almost disrupted our trip to Europe in June of 2000 before it even started. On that trip, we encountered one extremely rude Frenchman on the train from Poitiers to Bordeaux who belligerently refused to give my fifteen-year-old daughter, Anamaría, *her* seat on the train. In a small village on the Italian Mediterranean, our room at a local monastery, which we had prepaid before leaving the States, was much more "rustic" than we had imagined, and although it had a great view of the coastline, it was eight kilometers from the beach. We made the decision to "donate" our deposit to the monastery and find lodging elsewhere. With backpacks and a little anxiety weighing us down, our whole family walked through the town and found a vacancy well after dark. In another town, we experienced ATM problems one day. And we were all disappointed that the mountain we were staying on in Switzerland remained shrouded in clouds for the duration of our stay.

These and other stories could have plagued our memories of that once-in-a-lifetime adventure through Europe. If we'd had a different attitude, those inconveniences could have ruined our trip. The pilgrim heart looks to the journey with willingness, openness, and quite often a huge sense of humor. When an entire family attempts this sort of attitude, the blessings of the journey simply multiply.

8

Creating Home for Other Pilgrims

~ María ~

During our summer 2000 Jubilee Year trip to Europe, we spent a long weekend in Ireland. We had taken the ferry from Fishguard in Wales to Rosslare on the southeast coast of Ireland. Our trip was spontaneous, with no reservations made in advance, which can be risky with a group of nine—our six plus a niece, a brother, and a friend. After driving through the south of Ireland, with a stop to kiss the Blarney Stone (not that we needed it), we headed north toward the Cliffs of Moher. Darkness and rain set in before we reached Limerick, so we found a small village and headed to a bed-and-breakfast. There was no room for us at this inn, but instead of casting us into the wet night, the innkeeper spent twenty or thirty minutes on the phone calling neighboring B&Bs until she found one that could accommodate four of us and another that could take five.

We are all innkeepers. Our fellow pilgrims need places where they can literally and figuratively kick off their shoes, put up their feet, and lean back and rest their weary heads. And if one of the main purposes of pilgrimage is inner transformation, as "innkeepers," we must create places in our lives and hearts that are conducive to transformation, of others and ourselves. First of all, we must make room in the inn that is the heart. At first, maybe all we can do is reluctantly provide a little room in our messy stable. As we progress on our own pilgrimage, we learn hospitality from others. We hope to take that spirit home with us and, in turn, become innkeepers to other pilgrims.

Developing an Open and Vulnerable Attitude

The year that our son was a freshman at the University of Notre Dame, my good friend Judy Reilly and I decided to make a road trip to Indiana to visit each of our firstborn children—Judy's daughter, Alison, and Alison's husband, Craig, who lived in Bloomington, and Christopher in South Bend. As I think back to that week in April, I fondly remember countless moments of laughter and hours of singing together through many long miles in the car. Yet one of the things that Judy and I did that made the week-long trek much more than just a memorable excursion was to have a hospitable attitude, an open spirit, toward the surprises and unexpected graces waiting for us along the way.

From the beginning, we discussed the attitude and style of travel that we wanted to embark on together, transforming this "Indiana moms' trip" into a pilgrimage. For that one week in our lives, we didn't want time and limitations to define our schedule, as is often necessary in our work and family lives. We desired to be open to the small things we would discover along the way. Even as we set a travel plan for our destinations, first Bloomington, then South Bend, we chose to embrace each day as it unfolded before us. And we wanted any activity or side trip that we chose to have the potential of enriching us and our journey.

On our second day on the road, for example, as we crossed St. Louis, we veered off Interstate 70 to visit and pray together at the National Shrine of Our Lady of the Snows outside East St. Louis. Once in Bloomington, we spent several beautiful days discovering the university town and the surrounding areas with Alison and Craig, walking around the lovely university campus, visiting its museum, and enjoying a leisurely afternoon on the town square. On Sunday morning, we celebrated Mass with Alison and Craig at their home parish. On Sunday afternoon, Judy and I visited the Dagom Gaden Tensung-Ling Tibetan Buddhist monastery in Bloomington to participate in a teaching session open to the public. This ongoing "dharma discourse" on the teachings of the "graded stages of the path" reminded me that all of us, regardless of our faith tradition, are hungry for the light of God. Or as St. Augustine said, "My soul is restless until it rests in thee." As we left behind the hills and woods of the south for the flat farm country that is typical of the northern part of Indiana, we consciously sought to discover what was unique to this piece of God's creation.

I can honestly say that our decision to stop at Kokomo was based solely on the Beach Boys' hit song. Yet imagine our surprise as we learned that the city of Kokomo was the birthplace of many things, including the automobile, the pneumatic rubber tire, the aluminum-casting process, stainless steel, and the first push-button car radio. Before leaving town, Judy and I set out to find a historic covered bridge dating to 1875 that our AAA book noted had been moved from its original location to a local park. At Kokomo's Highland Park, we also discovered Old Ben, said to be the biggest steer in the known world, and certainly the biggest *stuffed* one! Old Ben topped out at 4,720 pounds when he slipped on the ice in February 1910, breaking two legs and becoming another casualty of an Indiana winter. Still within the city limits, we came across the "famous" Sycamore Stump of Highland Park, an authentically Hoosier tree that once upon a time shaded a local stream for an estimated *eight hundred* years before meeting its final destiny as one of the oddest roadside attractions I have ever seen.

As we continued to travel north to South Bend, Judy and I learned that there are more than 175 Amish settlements across North America—and that the northern Indiana Amish country is among the largest. So we decided to do more than merely admire the black, covered Amish carriages that we passed on the state highway. At the Amish Acres Historic Farm, we saw firsthand the beauty of Amish furniture, quilts, and other crafts. We visited Nappanee, home to one of the largest Old Order Amish settlements in the United States. We treated ourselves to a traditional Amish home-style meal in Essenhaus Village, home of the largest family restaurant in Indiana. And at the Menno-Hof in Shipshewana, we walked through a one-of-a-kind museum devoted solely to the story and history of the Mennonite and Amish people.

That was only the first half of our trip!

Having a hospitable spirit does *not* mean that you stop at every site you come across on a trip. But I use our "Indiana moms' trip" as an example of how to travel with a spirit of hospitality, of openness and vulnerability, an attitude that we can choose to have on any journey, regardless of its length or duration. At every pit stop or gas stop, there is grace to be found. At every scenic site—or even historical marker—there is grace to be found. If, God forbid, there is car trouble along the way, even then there is grace to be found. Grace is never scarce but always abundant—and God is always ready to supply us with our "daily bread," and more, if we ask.

The second half of our Indiana trip included several wonderful days at the stunning University of Notre Dame campus. During the day, Judy and I walked through the campus, toured the Basilica of the Sacred Heart, and walked around St. Joseph's Lake. We visited with Christopher when he wasn't in class, and we were even invited to be spectators of the first round of competition in what is reported to be the largest outdoor basketball tournament in the world. In the evenings, we celebrated daily Mass with my son and his friends, going to a different dorm for late-night liturgy every night.

On our last night at Notre Dame, I walked Christopher by myself back to his dorm room at Keough Hall following late-night liturgy, then met up once again with Judy at our room at the Morris Inn. After visiting for a few minutes, I confessed that I was hoping we could visit the grotto behind the basilica one more time. Without looking at her watch, Judy instantly responded, "Then let's go!"

It was a clear, cool, early-spring night in northern Indiana. The stars covered the firmament above us and lighted our path through campus to the beautiful cave of candles. Tucked into a secluded hill beside the lake, down an incline from the golden dome, the Notre Dame grotto was built in 1896 as a shrine to Mary. It is a replica, designed at one-seventh the scale of the original, of the grotto of Massabielle near Lourdes, France—the grotto where our Lady appeared to Bernadette Soubirous. I have never been to the Notre Dame grotto without finding a crowd praying and lighting candles there. But that evening, which by then had turned into the early morning hours, we came across the largest group of students I have ever seen there, except for football game days. Judy and I silently knelt together, and eventually, I walked within the grotto area to light a candle before we headed back to our room. It was easy that night to comply with St. Paul's mandate to "Rejoice in the Lord always" (Phil 4:4). I rejoiced in the opportunity to see with my own eyes how at home my freshman son felt at Notre Dame, to meet his community of friends, and to celebrate the Eucharist with all of them. I rejoiced in everything, from the weather, to the blooming tulips all around us, to the Body of Christ present and praying there. My heart rejoiced at being able to share that evening and that week with a woman of faith who calls me her friend and who constantly reminds me with her attitude to see the goodness of life, to live the blessing.

God's grace is simply amazing—and always surprising. All we have to do is open our hearts and our minds to it. Clearly, one of the gifts that Judy and I gave each other that week as we traveled through Indiana was the ability to allow ourselves to be spontaneous, to listen to what we normally ignore, to be open to ideas and experiences that were new and unknown to both of us, to discover our daily blessings together. We rejoiced in the little things and, in doing so, discovered that there are no little graces! Each day, we unwrapped unfamiliar and delightful blessings and graces that surprised us, like gifts under the tree on Christmas morning, on almost every bend of our journey.

As Meister Eckhart said, "If the only prayer you say in your whole life is 'thank you,' that would suffice" (Muller, *Legacy of the Heart* p. 129).

The challenge is to remember and to live out this prescription for life, this attitude of gratitude, in the day-to-day moments. But when we do, God's promise is clear. "Spirit itself invites us to be joyful, to be awake," notes author and therapist Wayne Muller, "to passionately and courageously allow this moment to live within our hearts, deep and full and strong, to allow joy, to become alive, and to celebrate fervently the gifts of the children of God. To know joy we must wake up, we must not sleep in our expectations and disappointments. Paying attention to every molecule that graces our body with warmth and nourishment, we give thanks for life itself" (*Legacy of the Heart*, p. 131). When we welcome each moment with a hospitable spirit, we move into gratitude, which breeds in us a true knowledge of joy. The Lord is near, the Lord is in this moment, St. Paul proclaimed. "Have no anxiety at all, but in everything, by prayer and petition, with thanksgiving, make your requests known to God. Then the peace of God that surpasses all understanding will guard your hearts and minds in Christ Jesus" (Phil 4:6–7).

Sometimes being on a trip or a vacation makes us more open to change because we are already outside our normal routine. Perhaps once we learn that we can be open to the graces that God has waiting for us *on a trip*, we can convert the practice into a habit and carry it with us into daily life. And when we do, we allow ourselves to taste a mere morsel of the banquet of blessings that God has waiting for us every moment of every day.

Making Home a Haven

One way Michael and I express hospitality is to make our home a safe haven, and even a second home, for many of our children's friends. As our children grew older, we wanted to create a prayerful home environment that not only nourished our children but also welcomed their friends. We agreed that it was important to share who we are and what we have in this way, although we honestly didn't know what we were getting into.

Michael and I hope and pray and work to make our home a welcoming place. And we consciously make decisions to encourage our kids and their friends to make the "Scap home" the place to hang out. We try to keep soda handy and invite visitors to whatever food is available. If someone drops in, we ask her to join us for dinner and partake of whatever we're having. We don't complain (at least not to the kids) about having to stay up later than we want because they are playing a game or watching a movie. When I drive up and see cars lining both sides of our cul-de-sac, I make a mental note to thank our neighbors—once again—for their patience and generosity. And when the question, "Can so-and-so spend the night?" is asked, unless there is a specific conflict, the answer will be, "Yes, of course."

This means that our house will not remain clean or orderly on a daily basis. I won't always like every person who comes over. I've had to rethink—and, at times, abandon—my sense of privacy and personal space. And sometimes I seriously ponder how to continue our family traditions when a crowd of five hundred is involved.

But I have learned to treat the visitors like my children, to ask them to pick up, even to clean up. And if it's time for night prayer, Michael and I invite whoever is over to join us in the living room. It simply makes sense to get to know our kids' friends, and when they are up late, I'm thankful to know that my daughters are often under our own roof.

Yet the unexpected surprise in this slice of my life has been the abundant graces I have received from our "adopted" children. In the past few years, I've gathered a bundle of blessed memories, like the shells I love to collect on the beach, from my walk as the Scap mom.

Sometimes their expressions of love are small but meaningful, like scribbled "I love you" notes left on my computer desk. I treasure the e-mails and the letters addressed to "Mamma Scap." And I still smile when someone volunteers over our dinner conversation to give one of our children a needed ride.

Sometimes their love is grand and formidable but expressed in small details. Early in the morning the day before my mom faced cancer surgery, I was startled by a knock at the door from seventeen-year-old Katie, on her way to work. Before I could say that everyone was still in bed, Katie began, "I wanted to give you a hug and to give you this." She opened my hand and placed a small cross in it. "I am praying for you," she added, then turned around and left.

When our son left for college, I didn't anticipate how difficult that new experience would be on the whole family. We had to adjust not only to his absence but also to the feeling of being a family of five instead of six, a fact we struggled to remember even when setting the table. Aware of this empty space in our home, Brian volunteered to be the girls' adopted brother. Whenever any of us needed to see a "boy" in the house, he made himself available to join us for dinner or just to visit.

And when I heard that SHINE, the Catholic work camp for teens, was in town and in need of help last summer, I asked the members of our "expanded family" if they'd be willing to go as a group. Thirteen generous teens, only two of whom I gave birth to, joined Michael and me in cooking dinner for the volunteer workers. There we were, our ecumenical family, gathered under the banner of the Scap home.

The loving surprises that I receive from our "adopted" children have been endless, and the graces abundant. What an unexpected and lovely blessing this community of teenagers continues to be in my life!

Making the Heart a Sacred Place

Simple words have the power to change your life forever.

We've all heard them: It's a girl. Will you marry me? Your son's been in an accident. I love you. I'm pregnant. I'm sorry. I miss you. You're worthless. You go, girl! Please forgive me. There is nothing more we can do.

A few years ago, my dad and I were called into a closet-sized room and told to sit down. "We found a large mass," the not-too-genteel doctor blurted out. "And I'm 95 percent sure it's cancer."

My dad reached for my hand and remained sitting in stunned silence. No questions popped into my head except, "Does she know yet?"

"She's not awake from the anesthesia yet," the doctor said, avoiding my eyes. "Do you want to be there when I tell her?"

I nodded, and he stood up to leave. "I'm sorry," he whispered as he opened the door and walked out of the room.

So began a unique and amazing pilgrimage of love, hope, anguish, forgiveness, and mercy, as our family walked with my mom through cancer surgery and countless doctor visits, tests, follow-ups, and chemotherapy treatments.

It is one of the greatest paradoxes of life that in moments of crisis, we often experience the greatest grace. Perhaps it's because we are able to surrender our wills to God's when we have nothing else to hang on to. Perhaps we are more open to the graces because we are more needy. Perhaps we are able to experience the depth and intensity of God's love when we hurt and suffer the most. And there are, truly, blessings in *any* situation, whether we opt to see them or not.

We hold the inner key that can transform our lives from barren to blessed. That key is an attitude of thankfulness or, as author Julia Cameron calls it, "blessing." In every event, in every circumstance, notes Cameron, "we have a choice of perspective. Faced with difficulty, we can choose between disappointment and curiosity as our mind-set. The choice is ours. Will we focus on what we see as lacking or will we look for the new good that is emerging? In every moment, however perilous or sorrowful it may feel, there is the seed of our greater happiness, greater expansion, and greater abundance" (*Blessings*, p. x). Ultimately, focusing on blessing reminds us that we are children of God and that our dignity comes from a divine source. "The key to practicing blessings," says Cameron, "is the willingness to accept the full value of each moment. As we are willing to allow each difficult moment to soften and transform into its inner potential, our hearts become hopeful, clear, brave. . . . As we expand our consciousness in gratitude, we become larger vessels for good" (pp. xi–xiii).

The word *pilgrim* comes from the Latin *peregrinus*, meaning "foreigner." We are foreigners, not of this world. When we put our day-to-day hope in people or in the comforts of this world, we are forgetting that, as Christians, we are traveling through this land, on our way to our true and eternal home. This is the truth that God wants to share with us. This is the love that God wants to lead us to. This is at the heart of my spiritual identity. And everything about my life, including experiences that I would never choose for myself, are guideposts leading me on my journey home.

"Our challenge is to learn to meet whatever is in this moment without condition, without comparing it to what should have been. Practicing nonattachment, letting go of our expectations and meeting the moment face to face, we are free to appreciate whatever is set before us, to drink deeply from what is alive and beautiful in that instant," notes Wayne Muller in his inspiring book *Legacy of the Heart*. "Unencumbered by our holding onto what should or shouldn't have been, we are free to be surprised by life, to experience the wonder of our life just as it is, with our sorrows and joys simply providing color and texture. When we don't know what to expect, we may approach even sadness with curiosity and an open heart. When we loosen our grip on our expectations, everything becomes a surprise" (p. 124).

It seems like another lifetime now, but in reality, it was little more than ten years ago. Michael and I were not at a good place in our marriage. A series of events, actions, and bad choices had dug deep wells of hurt and injury in each of our hearts and threatened to break our sacramental life. We went through several years during which we struggled and downright disliked each other. When I think back to those days, there will always be a pang of sadness and hurt for all the lost time. But by the grace of God and through much hard work on each of our stubborn parts, we not only survived but learned how to make our marriage thrive.

That was by far one of the most painful and difficult times in my life. I wondered every day how I would make it—*if* I would make it—through the day. And it was also one of the most grace-filled periods of my life. Yet it took my having to walk all the way to the edge of hopelessness before I completely surrendered myself to God with open hands and an honest heart. It was only when I was on my knees that I could finally open my spirit all the way to the graces waiting for me. And I learned that I could tell my heavenly Father what it seemed I couldn't tell anyone else. God didn't want my tough act. He wanted my broken heart so that he could show me love. He didn't want my pretending to be okay. He wanted my honest feelings, no matter how unholy, so that he could heal me. And so the psalms became my heart's voice: "[M]ake haste to rescue me! Be my rock of refuge. . . . Be gracious to me, LORD, for I am in distress; with grief my eyes are wasted, my soul and body spent. My life is worn out by sorrow, my years by sighing. My strength fails in affliction; my bones are consumed. . . . But I trust in you, LORD; I say, 'You are my God.' . . . Let your face shine on your servant; save me in your kindness" (Ps 31:3–17).

One of the graces birthed directly from those hard years was our renewed understanding of the eucharistic truth that we live through our marriage. Michael and I are Eucharist to one another. We are one body in Christ. And when we are faithful to the sacramental spirit of our marriage, we also become bread for our children, our friends, and our community. Our marriage is not only a gift of companionship; it is also the way God speaks to each of us, the human conduit through which Michael and I come to know that we are God's beloved. When we are hospitable—in each other and in each moment—our marriage is the way we discover who God is, here and now, and how God is with us and for us. This is both beautiful and, at times, quite daunting!

I'm not convinced that we would have ever understood and heard those truths in our hearts without having gone through the hardship of those awful years. And so if I had known then what I know now and had been given the choice to go through all the pain in order to be where we are now, I am confident that I would still choose to go through it. Not because I know everything will be "all right" but because I know, no matter what happens, I can throw myself into the arms of the one who knows me as I really am. I hope and pray to welcome God into my heart each day, to extend my welcome mat, completely, to the one who loves me most. I want to trust. I want to surrender. I desire to give myself to God as I am. And this is not only good enough for him; it is all he asks of me. All I have to do is choose to have a hospitable spirit, welcoming the dawn with joy as it rises before me each day.

I am invited, daily, by my Creator, to embrace the truth that I am God's beloved and that my God takes pleasure in me. Beloved! Let yourself BE-loved, God calls to me each day. But if I stopped there, I would eventually become self-centered and self-absorbed. Not only am I invited to BE-loved, but I am asked to BE-love for the people in my life. Compassion and hospitality are essential elements for a pilgrim. When I know in my heart that I am God's beloved, I become a natural reflection of God's love for every person I meet each day.

We are pilgrims on our way home. But we are never alone on the journey—this is God's promise to each of us.

9

Facing Our Obstacles

~ Michael ~

Our pilgrimage begins with the simple question: Who am I? As we go through life, we search for answers. And, so it has been for all persons across time and culture as each human heart yearns for the truth, beauty, goodness, and the transcendent. Pope John Paul II, in his encyclical *Fides et Ratio*, exposes the nobility of the human heart when he explains that "truth comes initially to the human being as a question: *Does life have a meaning?*" Even "a cursory glance at ancient history shows clearly how in different parts of the world, with their different cultures, there arise at the same time the fundamental questions which pervade human life: *Who am I? Where have I come from and where am I going? Why is there evil? What is there after this life?*"

The initial pilgrimage in life is the quest to find answers to these questions. To answer them requires a radical and concrete engagement with reality. We have to keep walking. It's the only way to move forward. Yet there are obstacles that frustrate the journey.

The Obstacle of Fear

We begin to truly awaken as we journey toward the answers we need. We become more aware of our own hearts and desires. But we also become aware of a disconcerting, and largely unwelcome, presence. Sometimes it is no more bothersome than a small pebble in our shoe, that nagging little doubt. Other times it is more like a rock that keeps getting in the way—the fear that keeps reappearing on the path. And then sometimes we find a huge boulder or wall in front of us. This fear is so big that it makes us doubt that there is any path at all beyond the wall.

When I was six years old, I had a strong desire to jump from the high dive of our local pool. I also knew the rule: once you climbed to the top of the diving board, there was only one way down. Attraction and fear filled me simultaneously. I desperately wanted to experience what I imagined to be the exhilaration of the jump (I wasn't yet ready to contemplate a dive). But what if the water swallowed me up as I gasped helplessly for air? For much of that summer, I distracted myself with swimming games and didn't express my desire to anyone. But finally one day, my desire overpowered my fear, and it wasn't enough to just swim around anymore. I wanted the high dive. When I reached the top and looked down, I was petrified. Of course, the lifeguard wouldn't let me climb down the ladder. I sat there in fear for a long time before taking the plunge. And it was every bit as exhilarating as I had imagined.

I now realize that the diver, like the swimmer, needs to surrender to the water. The danger of drowning is greatest when we try to fight the water, flailing and splashing. Since human beings are naturally buoyant, surrender is the safer course.

The same is true of the spiritual journey, but it takes courage to take the leap of faith, to step out on the pilgrim path. We can attempt to suppress the fears and questions or to distract ourselves from them, but ultimately we have to dive right in and submit to the process of dealing with those fears. Either we surrender to the call and follow the pilgrim path, or we succumb to the fear and turn away from the joy and wisdom that await us.

The Obstacles of Distraction and Worry

We westerners are obsessed with time. Daily "to do" lists, sorrow over "wasted time" and "lost" productivity, and frustrations over "interruptions" in one's daily schedule all powerfully suggest that time is a precious commodity that is slipping away into the past. The year that I came up for tenure at the University of Oklahoma, my prankster colleagues put time sheets in my mailbox as a playful reminder that if they voted me down for tenure, my life as a practicing lawyer would require me to account for each sixth of an hour.

We understand that every minute of every day of our lives brings us one step closer to our final destination. Time is like a superlong people mover that helps us get from one gate to another at the airport. In the terminal of life, there are only two gates: birth and death. While the distance between gate 1 and gate 2 is different for everyone, the speed of the horizontal escalator remains constant for everyone, moving at 86,400 seconds per day. We stand (or sit, or walk, or run), powerless to change this reality. I cannot awaken in the morning and say to myself, *I'll take it easy today and only travel 35,769 seconds.* Or *I feel great today; I think I'll put in a 97,889-second day.* I don't even have full control over *how* I will use this time. I do, however, control my *approach to* or *attitude toward* these unrecoverable 86,400 seconds. The businessperson who has his cell phone out and ready to call the office or a client the moment the flight attendant gives the okay understands this acutely.

The only way to work well with our allotted time is to be disciplined. Discipline is the best replacement for the distractions that waste our time. To press the airport metaphor to the brink of its useful life, it takes discipline to treat airline ticket agents and security personnel with respect and dignity when you are tired, the lines are long, and the flights are delayed. Some of us think of this as common courtesy, but it begins as discipline and, we hope, becomes habit.

We recognize the need for habit and for discipline the most in our failures. The string of broken New Year's resolutions testifies to the difficulty of forming habits that allow us to live disciplined lives. How many exercise and diet plans become history by the second or third week of January? Health clubs make millions of dollars every year selling "lifetime memberships" to people they know will use their facilities only a few times. I must confess to having had an embarrassing lack of discipline when it comes to computer games. I could go weeks without playing solitaire or free cell on the computer, but inevitably (usually in the middle of a writing project), my mind would suggest a short computer game as a break from my work. Sometimes (I don't pretend to understand the psychology behind it) I would binge, spending hours playing hundreds of games in a row. Afterward I would lament the wasted time. I had invested many of that day's 86,400 seconds poorly. Since computer games are not essential to living, I chose not to invest my time in attempting to form a habit of only one or two games at a time. I took the easier route and simply deleted the games from my computer, eliminating the temptation altogether.

Unlike computer games, diet, exercise, sleep, and spiritual health are essential to living and cannot simply be eliminated by pressing a button. For most of us, earning a living and raising a family are not optional either. In deciding how we approach our 86,400 seconds, we must prioritize and then develop disciplined habits to use the time well. One friend of mine made his physical health a priority. He joined a master's swim club and for years has gone to practice daily at five in the morning. The first weeks and months must have been agony as his weary arms dragged his tired body through the water, his legs too tired to provide much propulsion and his lungs gasping for air. But now the daily journey to the pool is almost as second nature to him as is treating a ticket agent with respect.

The pilgrim, no less than the athlete, needs to form disciplined habits to successfully stay the course. Distractions lose their power over us when we have good habits in place. Each pilgrim has to figure out for him- or herself which disciplines are critical at this particular point in the journey. Without building discipline, our steps become haphazard, and our pace will often slow.

Christ came that we "might have life and have it more abundantly" (Jn 10:10). One key to this abundant life is found in the Sermon on the Mount:

> [D]o not worry about your life, what you will eat (or drink), or about your body, what you will wear.
> . . . Look at the birds in the sky; they do not sow or reap, they gather nothing into barns, yet your

heavenly Father feeds them. Are not you more important than they? Can any of you by worrying add a single moment to your life-span? Why are you anxious about clothes? Learn from the way the wild flowers grow. They do not work or spin. But I tell you that not even Solomon in all his splendor was clothed like one of them. If God so clothes the grass of the field, which grows today and is thrown into the oven tomorrow, will he not much more provide for you, O you of little faith? (Mt 6:25–30)

I am forever anxious about any number of things: the safety and well-being of my children, especially since three of the four currently have driver's licenses; having a positive balance in my checking account at the end of the month; college tuition; the rising cost of medical care; and meeting deadlines, including book deadlines. You name it, and I have probably spent some of my 86,400 seconds a day worrying about it in the past few months. Often the words at Mass "protect us from all anxiety" pierce me with conviction or bathe me with hope.

I am also forever distracted by any number of things. When the children were younger, there were diapers to change, vomit to wipe up, mindless games to play, what seemed like weekly trips to the doctor's office, and months at a time without a full night's sleep. Now that they are older, there are multiple trips to drop them off, pick them up, or take them to the doctor or dentist; basketball games (this winter, two daughters, two teams, four nights a week); debate and acting tournaments to judge; and dealing with the emotional highs and lows of teenagers. Dinners need to be cooked, and meetings—at work, church, and in the community—need to be attended.

We have found that one calming influence on a life full of worries and distractions is the rhythm of the liturgy. The church lovingly requires a bare minimum of attending Mass on Sundays and certain holy days; fasting and abstinence during Lent; and at least yearly reconciliation and communion. The rhythms of the liturgical calendar, with Advent, Christmas, Lent, the Easter Triduum, Easter, feast days, and ordinary time, provide the backdrop against which the habits of spiritual discipline can be formed.

Those who are aware that life is a pilgrimage know that, with all the anxieties and distractions in life, these minimum requirements are not always enough to allow us to truly rest in God's love. Just as jogging for forty-five minutes once a week will not get you in peak physical shape, just doing the minimum will not get you in peak spiritual shape. The Church offers a treasury of spiritual opportunities to those who seek to rest in Christ's love. He says, "Come to me, all you who labor and are burdened, and I will give you rest. . . . For my yoke is easy, and my burden light" (Mt 11:28–30). Through the church, we can come to Christ in the sacraments, in daily Mass, in the various prayer forms of the church, in sacred Scripture, in the great spiritual masterpieces, in retreats, in service to those who suffer, and in many other ways.

One spiritual habit that I have developed is contemplative or centering prayer in which I meet the Lord in silence for twenty or thirty minutes a day. This habit has been formed in fits and starts since my teenage years, when my pastor taught it to a group of us. I was too young and spiritually immature to adopt it as part of my life in those days, but the seed was planted. Early on in our marriage, María acquired this spiritual discipline and through her I became reacquainted with it.

For several years, I wrestled with this prayer form; two obstacles stood between me and making centering prayer a part of my daily life. First, I tended to judge these sessions with God, and when I didn't *feel* any spiritual fruit from the encounter, I would get discouraged. Second, I would judge myself, becoming discouraged by the numerous times that I couldn't quiet my brain or that it became so quiet that I fell asleep. St. Thérèse of Lisieux, the "Little Flower," was instrumental in knocking away these obstacles. This doctor of the church, who died at age twenty-four, left us a priceless gift in her autobiography, *Story of a Soul*. In it, she describes her bouts with sleepiness while at prayer. When I slept during prayer, I felt like a failure, like Peter and the others who couldn't stay awake for even an hour with Christ in the Garden of Gethsemane. When Thérèse fell asleep, she slept secure in the embrace of the loving Savior. What a radically different perspective!

Thérèse, Catherine of Siena, my wife, and others taught me that in coming to the quiet, I am not engaged in a project, an exercise, a test, or a competition (as a high-school swimmer, I was often engaged in competition with myself as I tried to better my times). Instead, I am encountering a great friend and lover. The obstacles fell away. I continue to invest time in my relationship with María even if the previous encounter has been less than fruitful, my mind is filled with a million distractions, or I am so tired that all we can do is sit quietly together on the couch with me nodding off. Why should my time with God be any different? After all, he can take my burdens and let me rest in his peace. Today centering prayer is a well-entrenched spiritual habit in my life. This is not to say that there are not mornings when I wake up and prefer to read the newspaper rather than sit silently with God. The fact that there are mornings when sitting with Love Himself feels like a chore shows how very far I still have to travel on this pilgrimage. But He and I are working on it.

My 1,200- to 1,800-second encounter with God in silence every morning is not merely a respite from the day's burdens. As the encounter with God blossoms into friendship, my capacity to remain in God's love throughout the day increases. The spiritual disciplines that lead us to God's peace will transform our days, relieving anxieties and turning distractions into what Kathleen Norris calls the "quotidian mysteries." Teaching, writing, changing diapers, cooking dinner, and even participating in committee meetings become forms of sacred worship, an offering of praise and thanksgiving to the author of our lives. I should add that I know this to be true in theory, and I have been graced with a few glimpses of it in practice.

Christ calls to us and says, come follow me, stay with me, and remain—indeed, rest—in my love. Distractions and anxieties hold us back, preventing us from advancing on the journey. Our daily spiritual disciplines become a school for our lifelong pilgrimage of surrender to this One who promises abundant life. They help transform our *approach to* and *attitude toward* the whole 86,400 seconds in our day.

What if we could take a sabbatical from the daily distractions and anxieties, leaving them behind for a day, a week, or a month, taking time to delve deeper into the divine mysteries? The physical pilgrimage provides just such an opportunity, allowing a time for renewal, a deepening of faith, and a healing of the soul.

The Obstacle of Pain

Peggy Stoks's story, told in Jeff Cavins and Matthew J. Pinto's *Amazing Grace for Those Who Suffer*, provides an honest appraisal of the reasons we so often run from the journey. Her story is also a remarkable testimony of God's healing love for those who have the courage to embrace the journey. Peggy's grandfather sexually abused her from the time she was eight years old. For years, Peggy led a "normal" life, subconsciously suppressing the deep pain that had robbed her of childhood innocence.

Suppressing our pain is like putting something in a pressure cooker; sooner or later, it will explode. For Peggy, this occurred with postpartum depression, when she experienced "sleeplessness, lack of appetite, and bouts of terrifying anxiety" (p. 73). At the time, she had not made the connection between the abuse and her depression.

After lashing out at her husband in rage, she decided to seek the help of a Christian psychologist. A poster in the reception area captured the reason so many run from the pilgrim path: "THE TRUTH WILL SET YOU FREE, BUT FIRST IT WILL MAKE YOU MISERABLE" (p. 73). We are broken, with deep wounds caused by our own sin and the sins of others. As Peggy acknowledges, the divine physician could have healed her wounds miraculously in an instant, but he did not. It seems that most often his preferred method is to give us the grace to endure as nature runs its course. He allows us to fully feel the healing pain but gives us the assurance that Christ is walking with us on the journey. Peggy's doctor warned her that confronting her awful past was "going to be a walk through a painful and very dark valley" but that "much good [would] come of such a journey" (pp. 75–76).

him, I have one son and three daughters. *A Man for All Seasons*, winner of the Academy Award for best picture in 1966, which depicted the life of Thomas More, is my favorite movie of all time. I have belonged to St. Thomas More Parish in both Austin, Texas, and Norman, Oklahoma. Every week, I lead a group of law students at the University of Oklahoma in reading papal encyclicals, and we call ourselves the St. Thomas More Law Student Association. In the summer of 2000, we left Oxford early on the morning of July 22. There were fourteen of us—our crew of six plus one niece, a brother-in-law, and another family of six, all visiting us from Austin, Texas—on this particular Saturday journey from Oxford to London.

Upon arriving at the tower, we headed straight to Thomas More's cell. We were disappointed to learn that we would get a relatively short guided tour, leaving no time to tarry and ponder More's life. (In contrast, a visitor can survey Sir Walter Raleigh's relatively spacious and well-appointed cell at leisure.) After hearing from the Beefeater who kept those of us waiting for a tour in queue, we felt fortunate to get to see the spartan prison cell at all, if just for a short time. He informed us that the cell had been open especially for the Jubilee Year but was not generally open to the public. When we asked why, he told us that the British government had no intention of creating a Catholic shrine at one of its great cultural treasures.

As *A Man for All Seasons* depicts, the cell has a small window on the side of the tower that faces the river, and I could imagine that it was damp and drafty much of the year. Thomas More, who had been Henry VIII's right-hand man as lord chancellor of England, spent fifteen months in the tower after being arrested for refusing to acknowledge the king's supremacy over the church. Most of the English church hierarchy had accepted the split with Rome, but Thomas More, a layman, stood firm in his Catholic faith. On July 6, 1535, Thomas More was beheaded. He is reputed to have said before his death that he died the king's good servant but God's first.

After our tour guide finished his talk, my friend John and I lingered for as long as we could—only a minute or two—placing our hands on the bare, stone wall near the window, attempting to enter the mystery of this martyr's life, and praying for his intercession on our behalf that we might have wisdom and courage as he had. Even though we only had a few minutes within his last earthly abode, St. Thomas More stayed with me throughout the day as I reflected on his life and martyrdom.

St. Thomas More was well known for responding to early Protestant arguments against the church. One practice he defended was the spiritual discipline of pilgrimage, which had come under attack by Tyndale, Luther, and others.

The protesters argued that pilgrimages were corrupt, for various reasons: priests and shrines illegitimately made money off the pilgrims; bad priests led their flocks into idolatry, worshiping the ground and the images found at the pilgrimage sites; priests and pilgrims sometimes offered prayers to saints for evil purposes.

In his *Dialogue Concerning Heresies*, Thomas More exposes some of the abuses with saucy tales. He tells of one town's irreverence on the Feast of St. Martin. On that day, St. Martin's image was paraded through the streets. If the weather was fair, townspeople venerated the image by casting rose water and other pleasant things on his image. But if it was raining, the people brought out their chamber pots, emptying them on St. Martin's image. Thomas More also recounts the superstitious and wrongheaded petitions of women who prayed to St. Wylgefort, hoping that the saint would help them lose their worthless husbands. In addition to saying that even these "bytter prayers" (p. 235) could be answered in positive ways (through the transformation of the husbands, for instance), More argues that such abuses are beside the point.

He asserts that the proper question is whether a pilgrimage can be done well, not whether it may be done for evil or in an abusive manner. Explaining his reasoning, he says, "For if we should for the misuse of a good thing and for the evils that grow sometime in the abuse thereof, not amend the misuse but utterly put the whole use away, we should then make marvelous changes in the world" (p. 235, my translation). Should prayer and meditation on Good Friday be dispensed with because some people abuse the solemnity of the day by hunting? Do we throw out holy days because some people display lewdness at these feasts just as they do on pilgrimages? Should the Lenten fast be forsaken because some get drunk during these days, or should the drunkards reform their lives? Should the Christmas celebration be dismissed because of those who abuse it? Thomas More wonders if prayers to God himself ought to be suspended because some people abuse the practice: "Commonly when the wild Irish and some in Wales engage in robbery, they bless themselves and pray to God to send them good fortune that they may make good money, inflict harm, and receive God's protection from harm. Should we find fault with every man's prayers because these thieves pray for success in robbery?" (pp. 236–37, my translation). Thomas More argues that just as we ought to keep prayer, the spiritually vital practice of pilgrimage ought to be maintained despite the abuses.

The protesters also argued that pilgrimages were unnecessary because God was present in every place in every time. Thomas More agrees that God "is as myghty in the stable as in the temple" (p. 57). More also agrees that "no temple of stone was to God so pleasant as the temple of man's heart" (p. 57, my translation). But, once again, the protesters' arguments proved too much. In his wit, Thomas More revealed the absurdity of the conclusion drawn by the protesters by showing that their argument against pilgrimages could be equally applied as an argument against all church buildings. He pressed still further, asserting that experience proves that "those who are the best temples of God in their souls are also the ones who most often come to a physical building" to pray and worship (p. 59, my translation). In short, Thomas More understood that God is accessible everywhere but we still go to church and on pilgrimages because it is pleasing to God and helpful to our spiritual journey.

Whether we journey to a sacred place or simply walk through our daily routine, we have to decide if we will allow imperfections and others' arguments to keep us from the path. Some people will never understand why you would go halfway across the world to pray for healing, just as they will look at you oddly because you have adopted disciplines that they cannot imagine for themselves.

Your primary obstacle may be fear or pain, sin or distraction, or simply a lack of healthy discipline. But as you face each obstacle—as so many other pilgrims have already done—you can be sure that your steps will become steadier and your heart stronger. If St. Thomas More had not already faced the heresies that battered the church of his time, would he have had the strength to face a martyr's death when challenged by the king of England? Dealing with your present obstacles will indeed prepare you for the road ahead.

10

Returning Home

~ María ~

On the final week of our monthlong walking pilgrimage on El Camino de Santiago, I wrote in my journal:

Today we walked 14.27 miles, mostly in silence, and I was grateful. I enjoyed being able to "be" and to simply listen to the sounds around me as we walked—our walking sticks hitting the path; the birds; the roosters; the cows; the rhythmn of each of our shoes (Pat's boots and my sandals); the soft, gentle water stream that followed alongside our trail for part of the way; the wind dancing with the tall and elegant eucalyptus trees. . . . Pat and I decided tonight to get up tomorrow at 5:00 A.M. to leave by 5:30, in the dark, in order to have as much of the cool temperatures as we possibly can. That will also be a shorter walk than we've been doing, only ten miles or so, which means we'll be in Santiago by mid morning—on the feast of Corpus Christi!

"As beautiful and powerful as this setting has been, I find myself wanting to leave, wanting to go home, to be home," I added that night in my journal. "Lord, help me, remind me, to push my hat down and focus my eyes on each step in front of me, and not on the length of the steep road ahead. . . . I've had a line from a song in my head, 'It's the end of the world as we know it. . . . and I feel fine.' I am ready to complete this journey."

No matter how meaningful or how inspiring our pilgrimage experience has been, there is a moment when we are eager to go home. We have humbly given ourselves to God and opened ourselves to the pilgrimage experience. And now our hearts overflow with thanksgiving at the evidence of God's hand in our lives. Our spirits feel renewed and strengthened in ways we can't even name yet. We feel different, and we know at some deep level that we *are* different. It is time, and we know it. We are ready to go home.

Home is where the heart is. There truly is no place like home. Or as Mark Twain noted, "Home has a heart and a soul, and eyes to see with." Then why is coming home often such a difficult experience?

Any hiker knows that walking down the mountain is often more difficult than climbing it and almost always more exhausting. After hours of strenuous climbing and the inevitable natural "high" of completing the climb and reaching the summit, going down is a hardship. The body is exhausted. It is suddenly easier to stumble and trip. The legs feel like jelly, often collapsing beneath the weight of a worn-out, depleted body. We feel consumed, yet the reality is that there is a whole other side of the mountain that remains ahead of us.

Why should coming home from a spiritual journey be any different? We stood on top of the mountain of our experience, and we surveyed the land of our soul. From the summit, we could see much of the path we had already walked, and, in awe, we thanked God for bringing us there. We may not understand all that the experience has meant, the ways it has changed us, but we don't have to. We know it is time to go home. We're ready. But that doesn't mean that coming down the mountain is going to be easy.

Returning home from a pilgrimage is a bittersweet experience for me. I am aware that in many ways, I am leaving behind a better world, an ultimately more *real* world than my daily, "real" life. But it is a world I was allowed to dwell in temporarily—in order to experience it, not to remain in it. It was a gift meant to teach me and help me grow.

When I finally return to my family, the impact is like two major weather systems suddenly colliding over Oklahoma. My family has missed me, and they have a lot to tell me about themselves and about the time I've been away. In some manner, both they and I feel a need to tie together and connect verbally the experiences we've had away from one another. And I have so much to say! Besides the details of my journey, I want them to know how much I've missed them and how much they were a part of my pilgrimage experience because they are a part of me. I have experienced something immense and powerful. And I know that this experience affects not only me but the people in my life as well. In a sense, I have brought home and into our family a new baby for everyone to meet.

Yet as much as I want to communicate, I don't have words to accurately or fully describe this experience. And though I feel so "full" from it that I can't take into my system even one more drop, I don't even know where to start letting it pour out. So, often, I simply say nothing. I want to shout that I just feel "high" on God. Or that I feel more connected to, more aware of, the Holy Spirit in the mundane and simple parts of my daily life. I have seen amazing places and met incredible people who have showed me God in the here and now. I have touched something holy. How do I explain that I am different? I have been transformed by my pilgrimage. I am still me, only I feel more truly and fully "me."

It is natural to feel confused by an odd mixture of feelings at our homecoming. Leonard J. Biallas describes the feeling this way:

> We find it difficult to fit our "new" selves into our old environments. We feel the stress of not knowing how to adapt personal changes into our former lifestyles. We are discouraged when we compare our travel adventures with the pedestrian nature of our reentry life. We feel the dissonance that is caused by the incompatibility of our previous views of the world with our new experiences and perspectives. Our homecoming often involves disruptions of the social order, as we feel that family and friends are pressuring us into being the "same person" as before we went away. (*Pilgrim*, pp. 267–68)

Yet as one Chinese proverb says, "He who returns from a journey is not the same as he who left." Even though it is normal to experience difficulty as you "reenter" daily life, it is not a simple or easy process. Precisely *because* you've had a powerful experience, your path down the mountain to everyday life is a difficult one. In fact, the bigger the pilgrimage experience—in length or in personal impact—the longer it will take you to adjust. As much as you desire to connect with the people closest to you, you are worn down from your pilgrimage experience—physically, mentally, and spiritually. And only time and grace will rejuvenate you.

Waiting for the Lord

You may be home, but you are still a pilgrim. The journey you have just undertaken is a graphic demonstration—and a powerful reminder—that your whole life is a pilgrimage. While the journey itself may have been the most intense part of the pilgrimage, the coming home is its most significant part. It is at home that you will unpack the impact of the experience on your personal life.

As consequential as the pilgrimage journey itself was, the most important journey you make is the one that begins when you walk into your home and begin to struggle with internalizing the experience. This particular pilgrimage experience will not conclude until you as pilgrim have discovered a new way to live. You will, in effect, experience a transformation as you move from the physical pilgrimage to a spiritual, interior one. If the gift of the journey itself is to go and see with new eyes, then the grace of coming home is to continue walking. It is in your daily living that the graces of your pilgrimage will manifest themselves fully.

We are and we remain pilgrims walking toward God, who is the way. Yet how well and how soon after our pilgrimage we experience transformation is ultimately not up to us. Even as we embrace daily life with a pilgrim's heart, our task is to wait for God's grace to transform us. "Happy are those who find refuge in you, whose hearts are set on pilgrim roads" (Ps 84:6). As a watchman waits for daybreak, says the psalmist, so our souls wait for the Lord (Ps 130:6–7).

As we wait for the Lord, however, there are things we can keep in mind to enhance our awareness and to open our hearts to God's transforming work.

If you're physically tired and still suffering from jet lag, be patient with your body! Listen to its needs. Then as quickly as your body allows, create a rhythm for your day that makes prayer its centerpiece. It is in the silence of prayer that we will hear God calling us by name and that his words will take root in our heart: "I will espouse you to me forever: I will espouse you in right and in justice, in love and in mercy; I will espouse you in fidelity, and you shall know the LORD" (Hos 2:21–22).

The minute you enter your house from your journey, there will be much commotion thrown at you all at once, from doctor's appointments and broken washers to luggage needing to be unpacked. But before you open that huge pile of mail, before you check any messages on the phone, before you read and answer your monstrous amount of e-mail, take time to walk through the house that is your home and just take it all in. Walk and breathe. Stay quiet. Resist the urge to pick up or clean anything. Make yourself remain reflective for a little while longer. Be still. Listen.

Allow yourself time and space for observing, for weighing your feelings, and for noting your reactions as you reenter life in your home environment. Even though you will be asked a million immediate questions, wait a few days, or even a few weeks, to talk. Give your spirit time to digest and assimilate. Let it unveil to you in its own time the insights of your experience.

Bring the details of your pilgrimage that were especially meaningful or transforming into your home life. For example, if you discovered—or rediscovered—the beauty of praying the rosary on your pilgrimage to Fátima, make the rosary part of your daily life now. If you were moved by the way that volunteers in Lourdes take care of and pray with the pilgrims who are seriously ill, consider volunteering in your parish to visit the homebound and the sick. If your tour group made daily Mass a part of its busy schedule, why not continue that daily rhythm now? If walking awakened your spirit to the voice of God in creation, make walking a regular part of your pilgrimage at home.

Take out your travel journal. Your pilgrimage is *not* over! Write. Draw. Quote from a book or magazine you've read. Finalize your sketches. Make lists or notes. It doesn't matter. By opening up the journal and waiting, you place yourself in the posture of readiness for what will inevitably come out.

As Tolstoy heard in a dream at the end of his life, "See that you remember." Create a memory box, a collage, or a photo album of the pictures and mementos you brought back from your journey. The items of your creation and the act of "playing" with your memories are physical manifestations of the "new" now living in you. They are signs to help you remember.

Sharing the Experience

Eventually, you will know when it's time to start sharing your many stories. Your spirit will open up and sing a new song—and the words will pour out of you like poetry.

Make many opportunities to share your pilgrimage experience with the people in your life. When you give your daughter the keepsake you brought for her from Mexico, tell a story. When someone at the grocery store asks you about your trip to France, tell a story. When someone e-mails you that she's glad you're back, tell a story. Invite friends from church for a chat over coffee. Suggest to a friend that she host you, your pictures, and a group of common friends for a show-and-tell of your pilgrimage. Organize a formal evening gathering to share your experience with people from work. Whether it is one big gathering or many small ones, formal or informal, be willing to tell the stories of your pilgrimage experience. Be open to sharing. You are called to share what you have learned, to tell what you have experienced.

Let the physical things you bring back tell your story. Dirt from Chimayo. A rosary from Fátima. Holy water from Lourdes. A scallop shell from Santiago de Compostela. Holy oil from Brother André's oratory in Montreal. "Our pilgrimage compulsion to bring back relics from sacred places reminds us of our experiences of the sacred," notes Leonard J. Biallas in *Pilgrim: A Spirituality of Travel*. "Taking something home is a ritual action that somehow makes the connection with the sacred world come alive again in tangible objects" (p. 276). Let your stories about these holy relics proclaim to those around you how and why they are a physical manifestation of your sacred experience.

The story that you bring back from your journey is the greatest gift you are called to share, the "boon," in the words of author Phil Cousineau. Whether your pilgrimage was to a local shrine, to your grandmother's gravesite, to the hospital where you were born, to a Marian shrine in Europe, or to a holy site in Israel, the boon you bring back "is a presence in the soul of the world that can be sensed and honored and carried home in your heart," Cousineau points out in *The Art of Pilgrimage* (p. 218). The story "is the gift of grace that was passed to us in the heart of our journey. Perhaps it was in the form of an insight into our spiritual life, a glimpse of the wisdom traditions of a radically different culture, a shiver of compassion, an increment of knowledge. All these must be passed on" (pp. 217–18).

Like a personal relationship with a good friend, every person's experience of a pilgrimage is one of a kind. That is precisely why sharing your own pilgrimage story is so important. Even if you went on a pilgrimage with a group of people, no one else will come home with your particular memories, insights, or sense of awareness. And every time you tell your stories, you may discover something new, like how "insignificant" moments are often the ones that offer critical insight.

There will always be people who ask about and seem interested in only details and numbers: what year the apparition in Lourdes was; how many pilgrims visit the Washington, D.C., shrine every year; how many miles you walked on El Camino de Santiago per day; how big the city of Fátima is. Go ahead and answer the questions as best you can. They will help you see and define what is important to you and even assist you in putting together the spiritual themes of your pilgrimage.

Remember that you have no way of knowing how God will use your story and experience. All you can and need do is share it—as honestly as you can. "Our tale will be like a flint that ignites the hearts of those who hear it," notes Joseph Dispenza in *The Way of the Traveler*. "Our story is valuable, for it is the record of our self-exploration and self-discovery. And so we formulate the arc of our personal narrative. Others may find in it a route to their own salvation" (pp. 97–98).

It is natural for people to eventually stop asking questions, but that doesn't mean you will be done processing your pilgrimage. It certainly doesn't mean your pilgrimage is over. Just as you will sort through the mementos and clothes on your bedroom floor immediately after your journey, you will continue to sift through and look over the treasured memories of your experience for the rest of your life. And God will always provide the people you need to ask you the bigger questions: How did this experience change your life? When and how did you hear God's voice? What was the most difficult spiritual lesson of your journey? What person did you meet who changed you—and how?

There's No Place Like Home

I have lived in four countries, eleven cities, and more than twenty-three different houses throughout my life. So it's practically impossible for me to relate to the emotional attachment that comes with the saying "There's no place like home." Yet while my sense of home is not connected to geography, I can't deny the understanding found in the word *home* that is common to all of us. For example, to say that I feel "at home" with someone is perhaps the loftiest compliment I can offer.

At the end of our pilgrimage journey, we come home, both literally and figuratively. But it is to a home like we've never known, to that interior place where God already lives. In this new "place" the truths of our experience lead us to new understanding and to new knowledge of our-selves. It is here, in this internal home, that we see what it means to live in freedom—from illusions, from pretenses, from the material possessions that bind us to daily life. Because our physical journey took us to an unfamiliar geography, we developed new eyes that now help us see things as they really are. We feel uninhibited by the famil-iar. During our pilgrimage, we knew that what happened each day was completely up to God. And now, back home, we bring to the daily rhythms of life this new awareness.

God invited us to go on pilgrimage. "I will allure her; I will lead her into the desert and speak to her heart," pro-claims the prophet Hosea (2:16). And there, "She shall respond . . . as in the days of her youth, when she came up from the land of Egypt. On that day, says the LORD, She shall call me 'My husband,' and never again 'My baal'" (Hos 2:17–18). When we are open to the "daily bread" of our lives, our God is always faithful and always surprising. Our daily yes to the unknown and new is all that God asks of us, both when we set out on our journey and now. Through that yes, God blanketed us with overflowing blessings and graces for our pilgrimage. All we have to say is yes, over and over, yes—and thank you. Perhaps the greatest simple prayer, and one that I return to again and again, is attributed to Swedish statesman Dag Ham-marskjöld: "For all that has been: Thanks. To all that shall be: Yes."

In a way, we set off on a physical pilgrimage in order to remember. We remember that we already belong. We remember that home is within us, deep in our hearts. We remember that we are already close to God. We remem-ber that we can live a pilgrim life here, in our daily home. We remember that we are God's beloved, God's chosen.

Appendix A

Suggested Pilgrimage Sites for Christians

There are already numerous sources of information on notable pilgrimage sites. The places listed here are not necessarily the most notable or the "best." Nor are these particular sites rated higher by some divinely inspired counting device in their ability to produce miraculous phenomena, though many miracles have taken place at most of these sites. Not all, but many, of these sites and cities are in remote, hard-to-reach places. This, too, seems to be part of the pilgrimage experience.

What you find here is nothing more and nothing less than examples of pilgrimage sites—some national, some international—with a short introduction to each that explains what makes it a special destination for Catholics. These examples are meant to make you aware about specific sites, some perhaps new to you. But they are also meant to get you thinking about your own understanding of what constitutes a pilgrimage site. Where are *you* being invited to go?

Basilica of the National Shrine of the Immaculate Conception, Washington, D.C.

Located adjacent to the Catholic University of America campus, the Basilica of the National Shrine of the Immaculate Conception is the largest Catholic church in the

Americas, and it is the eighth-largest church in the world. The Great Upper Church can accommodate more than six thousand worshippers, and the beautiful Crypt Church can comfortably seat more than four hundred. The shrine is not a parish church but has been designated by the U.S. bishops as a national sanctuary of pilgrimage and prayer.

The mere magnitude is not what makes this church, the patronal church and preeminent Marian shrine of the United States, an incredible treasure. Dedicated to the mother of God and the Immaculate Conception, the shrine and its numerous chapels offer powerful places of prayer and meditation on the titles by which Mary has been honored over the centuries and across cultures. For example, the Chapel of Our Lady of Hostyn, also known as the "Czech Chapel," was dedicated in 1960 as a gift of Czech American Catholics. As the shrine's official description online notes, this chapel "illustrates the struggle of the Czech nation and its devotion to Mary. The life size figure of carved wood and gesso is a contemporary adaptation of the well-known original statue, crafted by Maria Grace Kanova, of Houston, Texas. Recalling the rescue of the Czech nation in 1241, Mary is shown with the Christ Child atop rain clouds; in the Child's hand is a bolt of lightning. The translation of the inscription on the face of the arch above the statue reads: 'Remain a Mother to your people'"(www.nationalshrineinteractive.com/Home/Home.cfm). The Czech Chapel also includes a bronze statue of St. John Neumann, a native of Bohemia, who was the fourth bishop of Philadelphia and the first U.S. priest to be canonized. The position of the St. John Neumann statue, facing the Blessed Mother, "suggests the bishop is leading the way to Our Lady of Hostyn. To the right, beneath a relief of the saint and set in the pillar, is a bronze reliquary with a relic of the saint on a gold disk encircled by garnets. The statue and reliquary are the work of Jan Koblasa of Kiel, Germany."

The shrine reflects the story of twentieth-century multi-ethnic Catholicism in the United States and the many cultures that define what is "American." As Pope John Paul II noted on his 1979 visit to the basilica, the shrine "speaks to us with the voice of all America, with the voice of all the sons and daughters of America, who came here from the various countries of the world . . . who came together around the heart of a Mother they all had in common."

With more than sixty different chapels and oratories, the shrine is also a symbol of the diversity of the *Catholic* (universal) Church. As a history of the shrine (National Shrine of the Immaculate Conception, "America's Patronal Church") observes, "Every stone and artistic nuance of the Shrine proclaims our nation's relationship with Mary, a spiritual bond formalized in 1847 with Pope Pius IX's proclamation of Mary as 'Patroness of the United States' under the title of her Immaculate Conception."

El Santuario de Chimayó, New Mexico

It is a simple adobe church perched at 6,220 feet in the Sangre de Cristo Mountains, off the "High Road to Taos" between Santa Fe and Taos (Highway 76)—a scenic route through old Spanish towns in northern New Mexico. Sometimes called the "Lourdes of America," El Santuario de Chimayó is a tiny church off the beaten path in Chimayó, New Mexico, harboring a dried-up spring in its earthen floor, where the soil is alleged to have miraculous healing powers.

There is no written history explaining exactly how this came to be. According to the Archdiocese of Santa Fe, the shrine was built between 1814 and 1816, and we know that the story of Chimayó as a pilgrimage site is based on oral tradition that has been passed from one generation to the next by the people of the region.

One tradition recounts that around 1810, on the night of Good Friday, Bernardo Abeyta was performing penances when he saw a light suddenly burst from a hillside near the Santa Cruz River. When he went to the spot, Brother Bernardo started digging with his bare hands at the site of the light, and he found a crucifix. Stunned, he left the crucifix at the site and called the neighbors to come and venerate the precious cross. A group of men was also sent to notify the local priest, Father Sebastián Álvarez.

When the priest arrived at the site of the crucifix, he picked it up and brought it to the nearby church at Santa Cruz, where it was placed in the niche of the main altar. The next morning, however, the crucifix was gone, only to be found in its original location. Three times the crucifix was brought to Santa Cruz, disappeared, and was later found back where it had first appeared. By the third time, everyone understood that it wanted to remain in the hill at Chimayó, and so a small chapel was built on the site. A letter by Father Álvarez in 1813 described "people coming from afar to seek cures for their ailments and the spreading of the fame of their cures," causing "many more faithful to come in pilgrimage" (Archdiocese of Santa Fe, "El Santuario de Chimayó").

Unlike other sites where miraculous healings are said to occur, Chimayó is not associated with a particular saint or with Mary. Approximately three hundred thousand pilgrims visit the remote site each year, with the highest numbers—more than forty thousand—making an Easter pilgrimage. Beginning on Good Friday and continuing throughout the Easter weekend, pilgrims from all over the United States come to the shrine and take away a bit of the sacred dirt. Pilgrims walk as little as a few yards or as much as a hundred miles. "Most pilgrims start walking in Santa Fe, twenty-seven miles to the south, but others come the eighty miles from Albuquerque, walking part of the way barefoot or crawling the last few yards on their knees (a common tradition in Spain and Latin America)" (www.chimayo.org/today.html).

El Santuario de Chimayó was a privately owned chapel until 1929, when a group of Catholics from Santa Fe bought it and donated it to the Archdiocese of Santa Fe. In spite of recent publicity, Chimayó remains a peaceful, meditative place. The church's protective outside wall creates an enclosed yard around the chapel, part garden and part cemetery, which serves as a passage to the shrine itself. Inside, the nave of the church is typical of mission churches, housing a main altar screen as well as additional altar screens set against the walls of the nave. The panelings, known as *retablos*, are traditional in mission churches—with images in bright colors painted on wood by local artists, often depicting images of local personalities juxtaposed against angels and well-known saints. The legendary crucifix that led to the shrine's creation still resides on the altar. Two images of the infant Jesus are honored at Chimayó, the Infant of Prague, shown in the clothed statue to the left of the altar, and the Santo Niño de Atocha, a statue kept in the chapel where the healing earth is found.

The prayer room, located in the sacristy of the church, is filled with discarded crutches, braces, offerings, and messages of thanksgiving, left behind by pilgrims who claim to have been healed or affected in some way by their visit to Chimayó. But pilgrims come looking for the *pocito*, a hole in the dirt floor from which the healing earth is taken. When I visited Chimayó with my friend Judy, what struck me most about the little chapel that shelters the *pocito* was the simplicity and informality of the low-ceilinged room off the main church. Judy and I were on our way to a Habitat for Humanity project in Colorado, where we were going to meet students from our university parish who were building a home during spring break. Our stop at Chimayó was a spur-of-the-moment decision that transformed our road trip—and in a very real way, our friendship—into a pilgrimage.

Basilica of Our Lady of Guadalupe, Mexico City, Mexico

Having been conquered by the Spaniards under Hernando Cortés ten years earlier, in 1531, Mexico was still in the early stages of incorporating the Christian traditions of its new Catholic rulers into centuries of Aztec culture, rule, and tradition.

On December 12, 1531, fifty-seven-year-old Juan Diego Cuauhtlatoatzin, a member of the Chichimeca people, was traveling from his home in the Anáhuac Valley to attend morning Mass in Mexico City when he was stunned to hear singing and his name called from atop Tepeyac Hill. Juan Diego, whose birth name, Cuauhtlatoatzin, means "eagle that talks" or "speaking eagle" in the Nahuatl language, climbed the hill and found himself face to face with a lovely lady who spoke to him in his native language. She told him that she was Mary, mother of the true God, and that she urgently desired that a church be built on the site where she appeared; she asked him to go to Bishop Zumárraga of Mexico City with this message. Juan Diego did as Mary asked. The bishop, who did not immediately believe Juan Diego, cross-examined him and had him watched.

Returning to the hill and to the lady, Juan Diego reported on his lack of credibility and suggested that the lady send someone with more influence to the bishop. But, unswayed, she urged Juan Diego to return to the bishop a second time. Still unconvinced, the bishop suggested to Juan Diego that he ask the lady for a sign to show that she was the mother of the true God. When Juan Diego reported this to her, she told him to return in the morning for this sign.

The lady told Juan Diego to go to the rocks at the top of the hill and gather the roses there. He knew it was neither the time nor the place for roses, but he went and found them, gathering many into his *ayate* or *tilma*, "cloak." The lady rearranged the roses and asked Juan Diego to keep them untouched and unseen until he reached the bishop. Once in the presence of Bishop Zumárraga, Juan Diego opened his cloak. As the roses tumbled to the floor, they revealed a life-size image of the Blessed Virgin, which had been miraculously imprinted on his cloak. A great mural in the renovated basilica commemorates this scene.

Central to the Guadalupe story is Juan Diego's *tilma*, which was woven from fibers of maguey and bears the image of the Virgin Mary. Juan Diego's *tilma* is enshrined on the altar of the Basilica of Our Lady of Guadalupe.

Juan Diego's importance is obvious to the millions of people who have knelt before the image of our Lady on Tepeyac Hill. As the only person in history to have been gifted by Mary with her portrait, Juan Diego is a reminder of God's message of love and redemption to all God's children, and in a special way to the indigenous and mestizo (mixed-race) people of Mexico. Like Bernadette Soubirous in Lourdes, in a worldly sense, Juan Diego was a powerless nobody, chosen to bring the good news of Mary's son to a class-conscious society.

Our Lady of Guadalupe was designated patroness of Latin America by St. Pius X in 1910 and of all the Americas by Pius XII in 1945. On July 31, 2002, during his pastoral visit to Mexico, Pope John Paul II canonized Juan Diego, who became the first indigenous saint of the Americas.

Pilgrimages have been made to this shrine almost uninterruptedly since 1532. On the site of a former Aztec temple to Tonantzin, mother of the gods, the Chapel of Tepeyac now stands, marking the place where Mary chose to appear to Juan Diego. A new basilica nearby, dedicated in 1976, holds twenty thousand people and gives an unobstructed view of Juan Diego's *tilma* with its image of Mary, and the altar. Between the altar and the wall where the *tilma* hangs is a space where the people can pass by to view the miraculous image.

St. Joseph's Oratory, Montreal, Canada

Alfred Bessette was born August 9, 1845, in Saint-Grégoire, a small town twenty-five miles east of Montreal, Canada. "His family was poor, like most of the French Canadian peasants of that time. His father was a lumberman, and his mother saw to the education of her ten children. Alfred was orphaned at age twelve" (www.saintjoseph.org/dynamic/section/brAndre/index.asp?Language=En). He worked as doorkeeper at Notre Dame College in Montreal and in

1870 entered the Congregation of Holy Cross, taking the name of Brother André.

Since childhood, Brother André had been devoted to St. Joseph, the patron saint of Canada. During nearly forty years as a porter, he fostered devotion to St. Joseph among the sick, for whom he felt a special ministry. Brother André would pray for the sick person and often rub the person with oil from a lamp that was near the statue of St. Joseph in the college chapel, and many were healed. As word of his healing ministry spread, the trickle of sick people at his door became a flood, and he became known as the "Miracle Man" of Montreal. He became so well known that secretaries had to be assigned to him, to answer the eighty thousand letters he received annually from people seeking physical or spiritual healing. "I do not cure," Brother André always emphasized. "St. Joseph cures." During Brother André's lifetime, thousands of people claimed that they obtained physical, moral, or spiritual favors because of Brother André's intercession.

Over the years, Brother André persisted in his deter-mination to fulfill his dream of building a fitting shrine to St. Joseph, a place so great that it would draw the atten-tion of all who lived in or visited the city of Montreal. His dream was for the church to be built on Mount Royal. When the owner of the land on which Brother André wanted to build the church refused to sell the land, the trusting Holy Cross brother simply asked for St. Joseph's intercession; as a symbol of his prayer, Brother André buried a St. Joseph medal at the top of the hill—a tradi-tion that has evolved into the practice of burying a statue of St. Joseph to obtain the saint's assistance in selling or buying a house or piece of land. Finally, in 1904, Brother André received permission from the bishop to build a small chapel, which was expanded three times to accommodate the growing crowds. In 1924, Brother André saw the beginning of the construction of the current oratory on the western side of Mount Royal, overlooking the city of Montreal, a beautiful and enormous facility that was finally completed in 1967.

Every year, following Brother André's tradition of hospitality, St. Joseph's Oratory welcomes approximately two million pilgrims who travel there seeking a haven of peace or a spiritual encounter. The oratory is recognized as one of the great spiritual sites of the world, a sacred presence in the heart of one of the world's major cities.

Brother André died on January 6, 1937, at age ninety-one. His burial had to be postponed for several days until more than a million people were able to pay him homage. He was beatified by Pope John Paul II on May 23, 1982. The oratory, which now houses Brother André's heart in a small chapel, has the official church rank of "minor basilica." It is considered the world's principal shrine in honor of St. Joseph.

Basilica Church of the Uganda Martyrs, Namugongo

Situated about seven miles northeast of Kampala, this impressive shrine commemorates the twenty-two Ugandan Catholics who were burned alive, beheaded, dismembered, or otherwise killed in 1886 for refusing to renounce their faith. There is a list of forty-five known Catholic and Anglican martyrs; however, it names only those who could be formally accounted for. It is well known that many more Christians were murdered here, their deaths unrecorded.

The leader Kabaka Mwanga II, who assumed the throne in 1884, was determined to rid his kingdom of Christian teachings and its followers and began the systematic killing of Anglicans and Catholics in his country. In his efforts to curb the Christian influence and regain the traditional powers over his subjects, Mwanga ended up adding more chaos to an already chaotic political situation. The kingdom was thrown into turmoil and civil strife—Muslims fighting Christians, traditionalists plotting against all creeds. During this time, Mwanga was briefly deposed, although he was able to regain his throne later.

Rather than deter the spreading of Christianity, however, the martyrdom of these early believers sparked the faith's growth. Christianity is now the dominant faith in Uganda as a whole. The twenty-two known Catholic martyrs were declared "blessed" by Pope Benedict XV in 1920; they were canonized by Pope Paul VI on October 18, 1964, during Vatican II—becoming the first saints of modern Africa. The first reigning pope to visit sub-Saharan Africa, Paul VI visited Uganda and the martyr's site at Namugongo in 1969. While at Namugongo, Paul VI designated a spot for the building of a shrine church; the church was dedicated in 1975 and has been designated a basilica church. Pope John Paul II honored the Ugandan martyrs with his own pilgrimage to the holy site in February 1993.

Every year on June 3, thousands of Christians make a pilgrimage to Namugongo, the specific spot where the martyrs died. According to officials at the Namugongo shrine, about one million people have made the pilgrimage to this sacred site.

Poondi Madha Basilica, Tamil Nadu, India

The tiny village of Poondi, flanked to the north and south by the rivers Cauvery and Colleroon, is situated in a lush setting worthy of tourist guidebooks on southern India. The state of Tamil Nadu, in fact, is an attractive tourist region in the southern Indian peninsula, known for its tropical climate, hill resorts, and ancient culture. Along with their ancient language, the Tamil have preserved and developed a rich tradition of music, dance, and art. Three major religions coexist in modern Tamil Nadu, and its Hindu temples and pilgrimage sites are both ancient and regal in their architecture.

It is hardly a coincidence, therefore, that the first Catholic missionaries to this region recognized early on the importance of pilgrimage centers in the Tamil culture and built shrines dedicated to the Christian faith. The well-known Poondi Madha shrine is in the Diocese of Kumbakonam, a predominantly rural diocese, which was founded in 1899 by French missionaries.

But the origins of the Poondi Madha shrine go back much earlier than its current diocese, to the early 1700s, when the Italian Jesuit missionary Constantine Joseph Beschi built a church in the small village and dedicated it to Mary. Father Beschi was a scholar of the Tamil language and a great devotee of our Lady. He wanted to build a church at Poondi from which Mary could intercede for the Tamil people and spread the message of the Christian gospel.

In the nineteenth century, including the beginning years of the Diocese of Kumbakonam, French missionaries continued spreading the gospel in the region. In 1930, the diocese was handed over to the local Indian church, and the first indigenous bishop, Monsignor Peter Francis, was chosen in 1931; under Francis's hand, the Catholic faith continued to flourish. Meantime, word of the blessings, miracles, and cures granted by the "Miraculous Mother of Poondi" continued to spread, making Poondi a noted and popular pilgrimage site.

The present structure, completed in 1964, is a mixture of Gothic and French architecture, featuring a row of statues of Jesus' twelve disciples, missionary saints such as Francis Xavier, and its founding Jesuit missionary, Constantine Joseph Beschi. Throughout the years, people of all religions have come to the shrine to seek Mary's intercession and to thank our Lady for favors received. The shrine to the Miraculous Mother of Poondi remains a popular and often-visited pilgrimage site attracting pilgrims from throughout India, a testimony to the early missionaries who proclaimed the love of God for all of God's children. The shrine was raised to the level of basilica by Pope John Paul II in 1999. Because the shrine of Poondi Madha, like most pilgrimage sites, is not easily accessible, the local church offers lodging for its pilgrims.

Lourdes, France

When one thinks of healings associated with a pilgrimage, Lourdes is the first place that comes to mind. In fact, the first thing that struck our family as we walked around the Lourdes sanctuary area was the notable presence of the sick and handicapped—at the daily processions, at the grotto, at the liturgies, on their way to the bath buildings. Because of the healings and cures associated with Lourdes, the sanctuary is organized with extensive measures aimed at taking care of the special needs of the approximately eighty thousand sick pilgrims who visit this remote town each year, including hospital-style lodging and a community of religious sisters, youth, and volunteers dedicated solely to the care of the sick. It was quite a moving experience to witness firsthand the personal care and tender treatment that the dedicated volunteers offered the sick or handicapped men and women of all ages as they were wheeled to Sunday liturgy—and the prominent place they were given wherever they were taken throughout the sanctuary.

It all began in 1858, when Mary came to this small town, with a population of about four thousand at the time, at the foot of the Pyrenees in southwest France. Our Lady chose to appear to fourteen-year-old Bernadette Soubirous, a girl who spoke the Bigourdan dialect of her region and who could neither read nor write.

Bernadette was born on January 7, 1844, to François and Louise Soubirous. Although her family experienced few hardships in the first ten years of her life, they later fell into dire poverty. With nowhere else to turn, the family moved into an old prison that had been abandoned and closed for its poor conditions. On February 11, 1858, Bernadette joined her sister, Toinette, and their friend Jeanne in search of firewood in the foothills. As they arrived at the nearby river, Toinette and Jeanne began taking off their shoes to cross the water. Bernadette, because she suffered from asthma, decided not to risk her health by exposing her feet to the icy water. As she looked around for a shallow place to cross, Bernadette suddenly heard a rustling sound of wind behind her. She looked up toward the grotto, where she saw a golden cloud enveloping a beautiful white-clad young woman with an azure sash and yellow shoes who was smiling at her. The lady beckoned for Bernadette to approach and signaled with the rosary that hung on her arm for Bernadette to begin to pray. After the recitation of the rosary, the lady disappeared.

On February 25, the lady told Bernadette to "go to the spring, drink of it, and wash yourself there," pointing to a specific spot on the ground where Bernadette immediately began digging—and a spring miraculously appeared. Mary appeared to Bernadette eighteen times at the Grotto of Massabielle, near Lourdes, between February 11 and July 16, 1858. Our Lady repeatedly invited Bernadette to pray, identifying herself in Bernadette's local dialect by saying, "I am the Immaculate Conception," words that the uneducated young Bernadette could not understand but that were very meaningful to the local priest. Clearly, the story of Lourdes increased the commitment to the belief in the Immaculate Conception of Mary, which had been proclaimed as official teaching of the Catholic Church just four years before the Lourdes apparitions began.

In 1862, the bishop of the diocese declared the faithful "justified in believing the reality of the apparition," notes the Catholic Encyclopedia, and a "basilica was built upon the rock of Massabielle" by the parish priest, fulfilling Mary's request that a chapel be built at the grotto and spring; Pope Leo XIII instituted a February 11 feast commemorating the apparitions. Bernadette Soubirous later became a nun, joining the Sisters of Charity in Nevers, France, in 1866, and taking the religious name Marie-Bernard. After battling illness the rest of her life, she died on April 16, 1879, which is now her feast day. Bernadette was canonized on the Feast of the Immaculate Conception, December 8, 1933. Her incorrupt body still rests in a glass reliquary at the Chapel of the Convent of St. Gildard in Nevers.

Since March 1, 1858, the church has recognized sixty-six miraculous cures from the waters at Lourdes, with another five thousand "inexplicable healings." Approximately five million pilgrims from 150 countries visit this town of fifteen thousand inhabitants yearly, making Lourdes one of the most important cities in France in the hotel trade—second only to Paris.

Fátima, Portugal

In 1917, during the First World War, the Blessed Virgin Mary appeared six times to three shepherd children near the town of Fátima, Portugal, between May 13 and October 13. One clear Sunday morning, Lucia dos Santos (ten years old), her cousin Francisco Marto (nine), and Francisco's sister, Jacinta (seven), were tending their sheep in the green hills of Cova da Iria when they saw a sudden flash of lightning, followed by a great ball of light that came toward them and transformed into a beautiful woman wearing a brilliant white dress. The lady, a rosary in her right hand, was smiling when she told the children not to be afraid. Lucia asked where she came from, to which she replied, "I come from heaven."

The lady instructed the children to come back to that same place on the thirteenth day of every month until October, and she asked them to pray the rosary every day. Mary's messages to the children during those months were mainly requests for the frequent recitation of the rosary; she identified herself to the children on October 13 as Our Lady of the Rosary. Speaking to the children during that visit, she asked that a chapel be constructed at that site, and she called the people of the world to repentance for their sins, asking that people say the rosary daily.

A crowd of approximately seventy thousand gathered around the children, but they neither saw Mary nor heard what she said to the children. Then our Lady performed the miracle of the sun. The sun lost its color, became a silver disk in a multicolored sky, and began to dance in the sky as the crowd screamed in terror, wept, and prayed. Witnesses saw the sun zigzag through the sky for ten minutes, stopping three times before assuming its place in the sky again. While the crowd of witnesses contemplated the sun, the three children received four consecutive visions: the sacred family, Jesus joyfully giving his blessing to the world, Our Lady of Sorrows, and Our Lady of Mount Carmel with a scapular in her hand.

The apparitions at Fátima were declared worthy of belief on October 13, 1930. Devotion to Our Lady of Fátima was authorized under the title of Our Lady of the Rosary, with a feast day of October 7. Francisco and Jacinta Marto, both of whom died within a few years after the apparitions, were beatified on May 13, 2000, becoming the youngest people to be beatified since the modern canonization process began in 1592. Lucia dos Santos, the last surviving Fátima visionary, is a Discalced Carmelite living in Coimbra, Portugal.

The sanctuary at Fátima, one of the most famous in the world, is a neoclassical basilica that can accommodate more than three hundred thousand pilgrims. Inside the church are the tombs of Francisco and Jacinta.

The Holy Land

Perhaps no other place in the world holds as much magnetism for pilgrims of all faith traditions as the Holy Land, an area that contains the actual places where Jesus and his disciples lived and walked more than two thousand years ago. Although my first trip to Israel was a press tour organized by the Israeli government to promote tourism, it quickly became more than that. Somewhere between fancy dinners and elaborate press presentations, my heart transformed from journalist to Holy Land pilgrim.

Nothing can accurately describe the powerful experience I felt standing at the Mount of Beatitudes overlooking the Sea of Galilee—or the spiritual awakening I experienced walking the same streets in Jerusalem that Jesus walked on his way to the cross. For the Christian believer, it is impossible to visit Nazareth, the site where the angel Gabriel announced to Mary that she would give birth to the Son of God, or to walk the hills of Bethlehem and not be inspired or challenged.

Human history in this relatively small area of the world extends back more than half a million years. Historically, politically, and geographically, the area we call the Holy Land is a very complicated place, perhaps moreso than any other region in the world. Throughout history, people from the north and south have continuously moved back and forth and across this tract of ground—a narrow land bridging the vastness of Africa and Asia. Many of the sites in the Holy Land hold spiritual significance for Muslims, Christians, and Jews, adding to the complexity. No other place on earth carries so much religious, emotional, and political significance for the world's three most prominent religions.

The Edict of Milan in 313, which ended government-sponsored persecution of Christianity in the Roman Empire, ushered in the first pilgrim boom in the history of the Holy Land, and churches began to spring up everywhere.

Pilgrims continued to come in increasing numbers until the Arab conquest three hundred years later, which made a pilgrimage to the Holy Land a dangerous undertaking. In the Middle Ages, the Holy Land once again became a magnet for pilgrims, and there exist many written accounts of pilgrims' experiences during this period. Since the creation of the Jewish state in 1948, the Holy Land, with its complicated mix of Christians (Arabs and non-Arabs), Muslims, and Jews, has experienced wave after wave of political and social unrest. Today it remains a dangerous and volatile destination for Christian pilgrims.

Custody of the Holy Land's special places has been entrusted to the Franciscans since the founding of their order. In 1217, they defined as one of their "provinces" an area that includes the Holy Land. Because the province included the Holy Land, it was considered the most important of all the Franciscan provinces and was visited by St. Francis himself, who made a pilgrimage through Egypt, Syria, and Palestine between 1219 and 1220.

In March of 2000, Pope John Paul II made a historic Jubilee Year pilgrimage to the Holy Land. His pilgrimage, the first papal trip to the Jewish state in thirty-six years, was a symbolic journey through the history of both Jews and Christians, reconnecting the fates and faiths of the Old and New Testaments. In a gesture that was both symbolic and concrete, the pope publicly expressed his hope for reconciliation and peace in the Holy Land, and he asked forgiveness for the evils that have been carried out in the name of Christianity against the Jews, our ancestors in faith. In a letter that he placed into a crevice of the Western Wall, a holy place of prayer for all Jews, the pope declared, "God of our fathers, you chose Abraham and his descendants to bring your Name to the Nations: we are deeply saddened by the behavior of those who in the course of history have caused these children of yours to suffer, and asking your forgiveness we wish to commit ourselves to genuine brotherhood with the people of the Covenant."

Rome

When official persecution of Christianity ended in the Roman Empire, construction of churches throughout Rome and the whole empire proliferated. And with the newfound freedom to practice their faith openly, Christian pilgrims began making their way to Rome to pray at the tombs of St. Peter and St. Paul. Rome today remains a major and important pilgrimage site, with more than fifty major basilicas and churches, and countless places of prominence.

It is impossible for any pilgrim to visit all the notable pilgrimage sites in Rome, and it is also impossible to list them all here. A pilgrim could spend days, even months, at St. Peter's Basilica and the Vatican and still not see or experience everything that is available. A small oratory was originally built on Vatican Hill at the place where the apostle Peter, at his request, was crucified upside down because he didn't feel worthy of being crucified in the same manner as Jesus. The most important relic in the basilica, therefore, is the tomb of St. Peter, located under the papal altar and containing the bones of the saint. Constantine replaced this oratory with the original St. Peter's Basilica. The current St. Peter's was rebuilt beginning in the sixteenth century and was dedicated in 1626. As the spiritual home for more than one billion Catholics around the world, St. Peter's is a beautiful and reflective place. Its amazing vastness and majesty have physically symbolized the glory of God for his church throughout the centuries. On its walls and through its atmosphere, St. Peter's reflects a glorious blend of human and divine history— and the presence of the Holy Spirit. As human and frail, and often inept, as its members are, it is nothing short of God's grace and divine presence that have allowed the Catholic Church to survive and thrive for more than two thousand years.

When planning a pilgrimage to Rome, a busy city of approximately four million people, pack your walking shoes and a good map. The people are hospitable and used to answering questions, most of the time quite patiently. There are countless high-quality guidebooks to this city of ruins and famous fountains, each of them offering detailed descriptions of its historical background, and its churches and religious sites, which house every-thing from saints' bodies and major relics to important works of art. Some of the notable pilgrimage sites in Rome include the Basilica of St. John Lateran, the Basilica of St. Mary Major, the Basilica of St. Paul Outside the Walls, the Sanctuary of the Holy Stairs, the Basilica of St. Mary Sopra Minerva, the Basilica of St. Peter in Chains, the Basilica of Santa Maria in Aracoeli, and of course, St. Peter's Basilica and the Vatican.

Among the numerous amazing sights that our family saw in Rome, two places stand out in my memory. The Sis-tine Chapel contains probably the most remarkable reli-gious art that I have ever experienced. On our Jubilee Year visit to the Vatican Museum, as our family walked into the relatively small private papal chapel that is called the Sistine Chapel, each one of us instinctively became silent. There are no words to describe the artistic sight that cap-tivated us. We separated and began to pace around the room, gazing in awe at the amazing sight above us and around us. Two hours later, we were still there, oblivious to the time. The chapel housing Michelangelo's wonderful frescoes of the Creation on the barrel-vaulted ceiling is still used for some papal functions and for the conclave, which elects the popes. On the end wall is the *Last Judgment*, a masterpiece of vibrant colors that will take your breath away.

Along and near the Via Appia, there are several catacombs, miles and miles of tunnels carved out of the soft tufa rock, which were the meeting and burial places of early Christians in Rome for five centuries. The catacomb of Priscilla, which is the one catacomb that our family visited, is not the most famous or the largest catacomb, although it is one of the oldest. The most remarkable thing about the catacomb of Priscilla is that it houses the most ancient image of the Virgin Mary—a fresco dating from the beginning of the third century. This unpretentious image of the Madonna, the first Christian, embodies the mystery at the heart of the Christian faith, the incarnation of the Son of God, born of a human woman. The simple but beautiful image painted directly on the wall of rock by the early Christians illustrates the importance of the mother of Jesus to the first Christian believers, who found it natural to honor the mother of their Savior.

One factor that contributed greatly to making our visit to Rome a true pilgrimage was lodging in one of the city's many convents and monasteries that rent out rooms for a very reasonable price, most of them including breakfast. At the Casa Santa Brigida, where our family stayed, not only did the sisters orient and feed our tired family every morning; they also reminded us that they were praying for us and for our pilgrimage experience—and even offered us tickets to the papal Mass for the Feast of Pentecost, an experience that will remain etched in our hearts and minds forever.

Santiago de Compostela, Spain

If any place has earned the right to be called a true pilgrimage site, it is Santiago de Compostela, the city and church in northwest Spain believed to house the relics of the apostle Santiago (St. James).

The road to Santiago de Compostela, known as El Camino de Santiago ("the Way of St. James") is actually not one single path. Since the Middle Ages, pilgrims from all over Europe have traveled toward the city of Santiago de Compostela, most of them eventually joining one of four major French roads that funnel toward the Pyrenees, the Iberian Peninsula's northern gate. Once in Spain, however, the principal roads merge into one path as they drop south out of the mountains and then head straight west to Santiago de Compostela. Most modern pilgrims walk this path, the *Camino francés* (known as the "French Way"), often beginning at Saint-Jean-Pied-de-Port, where many of the French trails converge. This route crosses the Pyrenees to Roncesvalles, the first Spanish town on El Camino. There are numerous books and Internet sites on El Camino de Santiago, some offering practical information for the would-be pilgrim, many relating personal stories of a pilgrimage to Santiago de Compostela.

During the Middle Ages, El Camino de Santiago became one of the three major Christian pilgrimage routes. It follows a Roman trade route nicknamed *la voje ladee* ("the Milky Way"), and even today, the Spanish refer to El Camino as the Milky Way because once there were as many pilgrims as there are stars in the sky. The Italian poet Dante Alighieri once wrote that the only true pilgrim is the one who walks to the tomb of Santiago in Compostela.

El Camino remains the most popular long-distance trail in Europe, winding its way through France and the heights of the Pyrenees, to the crop fields and wildernesses of the Spanish north, to the gently rolling fields and eucalyptus forests of Galicia. Thousands of pilgrims from all over the world complete all or some of the approximately five hundred miles of el Camino every year, most of them walking. But others also travel by bicycle, by car, by horseback, and even by wheelchair. According to figures published by the diocese of Santiago, in 2003, 74,614 pilgrims received the official *Compostela*, the traditional Latin certificate of pilgrimage for those who declare a spiritual motivation and who have walked or ridden on horseback the last one hundred kilometers, or cycled the last two hundred kilometers, to Santiago de Compostela.

The reasons for walking the road to Santiago de Compostela are as varied and numerous as the pilgrims who have walked the path. Clearly, something invites both believers and nonbelievers to grab their backpacks, put on the scallop shell—the universal insignia of a Santiago de Compostela pilgrim—and take on the challenge. While the first pilgrims on the road to Santiago de Compostela may have encountered a rather primitive and uncivilized experience, today's journey is much more organized, although still a true physical and spiritual challenge. A pilgrim's *credencial* (or pilgrim "passport") and scallop shell identify the walker or biker as an official pilgrim. The *credencial* also allows the pilgrim access to lodging in the *refugios*—very cheap, simple hostels along the Camino, reserved only for pilgrims on their way to Santiago de Compostela.

What If I Can't Travel Far?

The time or money necessary, or other considerations, may limit a pilgrim's ability to travel to the "big" national and international Catholic pilgrimage sites. Using examples from Oklahoma, where parts of the state are as low as 3 percent Catholic, this section challenges you to seek out pilgrimage sites in your own backyard. Listed here are the ten places in Oklahoma designated by the Archdiocese of Oklahoma City as pilgrimage destinations for the Jubilee Year 2000.

Holy Trinity Church and Cemetery, Okarche

On April 19, 1892, the town of Okarche, located on the Chisholm Trail and in the area of the Cheyenne-Arapaho Reservation, was opened for settlement. A year later, plans were drawn up for the first Catholic chuch building, and a parish school opened in 1897. The church is "well known for the beauty of its architecture, and it contains numerous works of artistic value—including an ornate high altar, the original baptistery of alabaster and bronze, and intricate stained-glass windows." The Holy Trinity Church cemetery is the burial place of its most famous son, Father Stanley Rother, who was martyred for the faith in Guatemala on July 28, 1981. A bronze relief of Father Rother stands in the church sanctuary.

Cathedral of Our Lady of Perpetual Help, Oklahoma City

Founded in 1919 by the first bishop of Oklahoma, Theophile Meerschaert, Our Lady of Perpetual Help was named the cathedral for the diocese in 1931. The cathedral is designed in the Romanesque style, with a large central rectangular space, or nave, and side aisles created from rows of columns that support the ceiling. High above the west entrance is the rose window, containing a representation of the mysteries of the rosary. The other stained-glass windows depict scenes from the life of the Blessed Virgin Mary, including Mary and her mother, Mary's engagement to Joseph, the miracle at Cana, and Mary's crowning as Queen of Heaven.

In 1975, thirty Vietnamese families seeking refuge from religious and political persecution found their way to the Cathedral of Our Lady of Perpetual Help, and the Vietnamese population in the area has been growing ever since. Our Lady of Perpetual Help has an active ministry to its Vietnamese parishioners. It has a Vietnamese Mass every Sunday, and it assists the Vietnamese community in nurturing its observance of cultural holidays within the Catholic liturgical calendar.

St. Joseph's Old Cathedral, Oklahoma City

Shortly after the Land Run of 1889, which founded Oklahoma City, a group of Catholics gathered to choose a site for the first Catholic church. They chose Blue Hill, the highest hill in the new settlement, and the frame church's steeple was topped with a cross on July 31, 1889. St. Joseph's was the first church of any denomination built in Oklahoma City. The parish moved into its current, brick building in 1903, and Oklahoma was raised to the level of a diocese in 1905.

The 1995 bombing of the Alfred P. Murrah Federal Building caused great damage to St. Joseph's Old Cathedral. The church underwent extensive interior and exterior restoration and was rededicated on December 1, 1996. In 1998, a special monument on the church grounds was dedicated by the archdiocese in honor of those who died on April 19, 1995. The statue of Jesus, titled *And Jesus Wept*, is located behind the church building, on the corner facing the Oklahoma City National Memorial and the site of the bombing. The monument was created to express remembrance, reflection, and faith in the enduring presence of Christ, especially in a time of need.

St. Gregory's Abbey Chapel, Shawnee

On October 12, 1875, two Benedictine monks of the Abbey of Pierre-qui-Vire in France arrived to take up permanent residence in Indian Territory. By 1877, they were at work among the Potawatomi Indians, having established a monastery and school at Sacred Heart Mission. Within five years, Benedictine priests from the monastery had opened more than a dozen parishes in Indian Territory, thus firmly establishing the Catholic Church in Oklahoma. When the monastery and school were destroyed by fire in 1901, the school was moved to a more populous location. The monastery relocated to this new site in 1929, with the new abbey and abbey church both dedicated and consecrated in 1955. Its sister institution, St. Gregory's University, is run by the Benedictine brothers and priests and is the only Catholic university in Oklahoma. The Benedictine brothers and priests at St. Gregory's welcome visitors to celebrate the Liturgy of the Hours with them.

Corpus Christi Church, Oklahoma City

An important part of the history and identity of Corpus Christi Parish was the church of St. Peter Claver, located in a predominantly African American Catholic community. Beginning in the 1950s, African American families began moving into Corpus Christi Parish and sending their children to Corpus Christi Catholic School. The parishes of Corpus Christi and St. Peter Claver eventually merged, making Corpus Christi a predominantly African American parish. Today Corpus Christi Church is a spiritual house of worship for all who enter, regardless of race.

Little Flower Church, Oklahoma City

When the Discalced Carmelite Fathers were expelled from Mexico in the 1914 persecutions of the church, they found their way to Oklahoma City. By 1922, they had established their work among the city's Spanish-speaking residents. A beautiful church dedicated to Our Lady of Mount Carmel was built in 1926. In 1928, the church's ornate high altar was dedicated to our Lady and to St. Thérèse of Lisieux, the "Little Flower." It became a Carmelite provincial house in 1936. The number of Spanish speakers who have settled in Oklahoma in recent years has caused the parish to grow in huge leaps; today more than two thousand people participate in Mass each Sunday.

Resurrection Cemetery Chapel, Oklahoma City

A Catholic cemetery is more than just a burial ground. It is a religious and sacred institution, a "reliquary of saints" waiting for that final, glorious moment of the Resurrection, the unification of the body and the soul in Christ. Resurrection Cemetery Chapel was built in 1962 at the center of the cemetery. The chapel floor, in the design of a Greek cross, has floor crypts—a burial practice that began hundreds of years ago, when the nobility, seeking to be close to God in death, would bequeath large sums of money to build churches in which their remains would be entombed. Four bishops of Oklahoma are entombed at Resurrection Cemetery Chapel: Theophile Meerschaert, Francis Clement Kelley, Eugene Joseph McGuinness, and Victor Joseph Reed.

Archdiocesan Shrine of Our Lady of Fátima, Bison

The erection of the Shrine of Our Lady of Fátima in 1951 was marked from start to finish by feast days of the Blessed Virgin Mary. On September 8, the Feast of the Nativity of Mary, men from St. Joseph Parish in Bison hauled native limestone from Burbank, Oklahoma. Construction began on October 11, the Feast of the Maternity of Mary. The completed shrine was dedicated on December 8, the Feast of the Immaculate Conception.

On November 24, 1992, the shrine was destroyed by fire, with only the stone shell and fire-blackened statues remaining. In November 1993, restoration work was begun by men of the parish who volunteered their labor. The statues were also restored, and faceted glass windows were added, depicting the miracle of the sun, which occurred on October 13, 1917, in Fátima, Portugal, where Mary appeared to three shepherd children. The shrine is open twenty-four hours a day, seven days a week.

St. Mary's Church, Guthrie

Shortly after the Land Run of 1889, Mass was offered in Guthrie—the city that eventually became the first capital of Oklahoma. When Bishop Theophile Meerschaert arrived in 1891, St. Mary's Church became his official residence and remained so until the bishop moved to Oklahoma City in 1905, the same year that Oklahoma was named a diocese. St. Mary's Church was the site of

Oklahoma's first priestly ordination, that of Father William Henry Kercham in 1892. And it was the site of the first religious profession, by Sister M. Genevieve Smith, O.S.B. The original building was torn down to make way for the current church, built in 1920.

National Shrine of the Infant Jesus of Prague

The town of Prague, Oklahoma, was settled by a group of Czech Catholics. As the town grew, it became evident that they needed a church larger than their small wooden building. The new church, St. Wenceslaus, was dedicated in 1909 but was destroyed by a tornado in 1919. A brick church was built that same year, and it served the community until after the Second World War, when once again, a larger church was needed. In 1948, Father George Johnson came to Oklahoma to build a new church for the parish, but he became discouraged by the lack of donations. Father Johnson began to pray to the Infant of Prague, and before long, sufficient donations were received to build the present church. The church was dedicated in 1949 and named the National Shrine of the Infant Jesus of Prague; it receives hundreds of pilgrims and tourists every year. It is open daily, from sunrise to sunset.

Appendix B

Questions and Topics for Journaling

- Describe in as much detail as you can a moment that became important to you during your pilgrimage, with special attention to unexpected events and sights.

- Visualize a specific door you have seen during your journey. It doesn't matter if it's simple and ordinary, or exotic and regal. Imagine the door as a threshold moment in your life. How are this particular door and its qualities a metaphor for what's happening inside you?

- Pick one of the mementos you brought back for yourself and write about its significance.

- Pick one of the mementos you brought back for someone else and write a letter explaining why you picked it for your friend. (You don't have to send the letter.)

- Write a blessing for the places you have walked on your journey—streets and towns, shrines or chapels, hotel rooms, meeting rooms, shops, museums and memorials. Don't forget to include a blessing for pilgrims who will walk in your footsteps.

- Draw or imagine a personal and colorful patchwork quilt. For each patch in the quilt, write a short description of a moment or image that held special spiritual significance for you.

- Pick and write about an animal or an item in nature (a tree, a rose) that exemplifies the metamorphoses you feel inside.

- Compose a psalm (of thanksgiving, of praise, of supplication) to describe your pilgrimage experience.

- Compose a chronology of events, from the time you left home to the time you returned. Then write a story of your pilgrimage using the listed details. You are also the editor, so include or leave out whatever you want.

- Pick one of the following moments from your pilgrimage and write about it: the funniest moment; the hardest moment; the most significant moment; the most unexpected moment; your favorite moment.

- (Adapted from Joseph Dispenza's *The Way of the Traveler*) Make a list of the people you encountered on your pilgrimage. Next to each name, write an adjective or two describing that person or your encounter with him or her. Review the words you have written, allowing the list to show you a pattern, an image, a recurring theme.

Appendix C

María and Michael's "Top Ten" Suggestions

1. As much as is realistically possible, involve in the preparations and decisions everyone in your family who will be going on the pilgrimage. For example, the Christmas before our Jubilee Year family pilgrimage, each member of the family received as a gift a guidebook to his or her favorite country or city among those we would be visiting. That person was in charge of reading and sharing information with the rest of us.

2. Think through what prayer material (prayer books, rosary, etc.) you want to bring with you. If you are backpacking, you will want to keep the load light, so you might bring a miniature New Testament with Psalms. For our summerlong pilgrimage, it made sense for our family to bring three small paperback copies (shared by the six of us) of the Night Prayer from the Liturgy of the Hours to say as a family before turning out the lights.

3. Learn about other people's experiences on the particular pilgrimage you will be making, whether by talking with people you know or by reading someone's book or Web site. Learn from their mistakes and brilliant moments. Use what you learn to make a list of things you want to emulate or avoid.

4. Surf the Web. You can find churches and other potential pilgrimage sites, Mass schedules, train schedules and fares, museum hours, and other useful information on the Internet. You might find message boards for people who have already made, or are planning to make, a pilgrimage to the place you will be visiting. And Web sites such as Rick Steves's have helpful information on packing, exchanging currency, and just about anything else.

5. If you are striking out on your own, do enough research to become familiar with the logistics of your trip. Then consult a travel agent. With your base of knowledge, you will be able to tell whether the agent knows what she is doing, and you will develop a sense of her strengths and weaknesses. Use her when it is helpful and make other arrangements when it is not. For our Jubilee Year pilgrimage to Europe, we saved four hundred dollars per plane ticket (times six tickets) because our travel agent, who had informed us of the benefits and drawbacks of using a ticket consolidator, worked through a reputable consolidator. We also bought some of our train travel (a Eurail pass) from her, but we knew that we could purchase additional train travel at a cheaper fare on location. In the end, nothing substitutes for your own research.

6. In addition to purchasing guidebooks about your destination, buy or borrow books or movies about the place or the people associated with it. For example, watch *The Song of Bernadette* if you are going to Lourdes. Read G. K. Chesterton's biography (or

another biography) of St. Francis if you are going to Assisi.

7. If you are traveling to a popular destination, check to see if you can purchase any necessary admissions tickets online before you leave home. (We would have spent hours in the hot sun waiting to enter Florence's top two art museums if someone had not given us this tip.)

8. Remember that a pilgrimage is not a rat-race tourist vacation during which you have to see it all. Make sure that the pace is balanced enough so you have the time to be still and appreciate God's presence. Make time for leisurely meals and try to alternate days with hectic paces and days with more leisurely paces.

9. Buy a journal for each member of the family who will be going so that each of you can write down your own reflections about the experience.

10. Don't forget to bring the postal and e-mail addresses of your friends and family. During our summer in Europe, we would occasionally stop at an Internet café and send either a personal or a mass e-mail to family and friends so that they could share some of the journey with us. If you have a digital camera, you can even send pictures. And, with all the junk that comes in the mail, your friends and family will enjoy receiving a postcard.

Bonus:

11. Make sure all your travel documents, including passports, are secured well in advance. And make a

photocopy of each important document just in case you lose the original.

Appendix D

Travel Agencies, Pilgrim Associations, and Helpful Web Sites

This list is for your information; we are not recommending any particular travel agency. We have probably left out some very good travel agencies and pilgrim associations, and we are sorry for that.

Travel Agencies and Pilgrim Associations

American Association of Friends of the Road
    to Santiago
2501 Kingstown Rd.
Kingston, RI 02881
e-mail: dgitlitz@aol.com
Web site: www.geocities.com/friends_usa_santiago

Best Catholic Pilgrimages
phone: 800-908-BEST
e-mail: info@bestcatholic.com
Web site: www.eholy.com

Canterbury Tours
7582 N. Broadway
Red Hook, NY 12571
phone: 845-758-2336 or 800-653-0017
fax: 845-758-5348
e-mail: info@canterburytours.com
Web site: www.canterburytours.com

Catholic Travel Centre
4444 Riverside Dr., Suite 301
Burbank, CA 91505
phone: 818-848-9449 or 800-553-5233
fax: 818-848-0712
e-mail: info@ctctwt.com
Web site: www.gocatholictravel.com

Confraternity of St. James
27 Blackfriars Rd.
London SE1 8NY
England
phone: +44 (0)20-7928-9988
fax: +44 (0)20-7928-2844
e-mail: office@csj.org.uk
Web site: www.csj.org.uk

ITS International Tours
3945 N. I-10 Service Rd., Suite 200
Metairie, LA 70002
phone: 504-831-0843 or 800-892-7729
fax: 504-837-2920
e-mail: itstours@itstours.com
Web site: www.itstours.com

Journeys Unlimited
494 8th Ave.
New York, NY 10001
phone: 212-594-8787 or 800-486-8359
fax: 212-594-7073
e-mail: journeys@ist-tours.com
Web site: www.journeys-unlimited.com

Pentecost Tours
P.O. Box 280
Batesville, IN 47006-0280
phone: 812-933-0730 or 800-713-9800
fax: 812-934-5714
e-mail: pentecost@seidata.com,
      gary.foster@pentecost tours.com
Web site: www.pentecosttours.com

Regina Caeli
2731 Salzedo St.
Coral Gables, FL 33134
phone: 305-442-7340

Regina Tours
494 8th Avenue, Suite 2200
New York, NY 10001
phone: 212-594-8787 or 800-CATHOLIC
fax: 212-594-7073
email: regina@groupist.com
Web site: www.regina-tours.com

Unitours
3010 Westchester Ave.
Purchase, NY 10577
phone: 914-253-9446 or 800-777-7432
fax: 914-253-9001
e-mail: info@unitours.com
Web site: www.unitours.com

Helpful Web Sites

www.pilgrimsprogress.org.uk
A Web site designed as a guide on the concept of pilgrimage, offering historical background, practical information, and links to pilgrimage sites and shrines.

www.catholicshrines.net
A state-by-state listing of various Catholic shrines in the United States, including their telephone numbers and directions to each.

www.eholy.com/best/holy-shrines.shtml
Information on the shrines of Lourdes, Fátima, and Guadalupe.

www.masstimes.org
Mass times by city and ZIP code for Catholics traveling in the United States.

www.monasteriesofspain.com
Web site for Eileen Barish's *Lodging in Spain's Monasteries*.

www.monasteriesofitaly.com
Web site for Eileen Barish's *Lodging in Italy's Monasteries*.

www.archicompostela.org/Peregrinos/Inglés/Peregrinsantiago.htm
PLEASE NOTE: this Web site can only be accessed by making sure that the word *inglés* (as is used in "Inglés" in the Web address) has its proper Spanish accent over the *e*. This is the Official Web site of the Archdiocese of Santiago de Compostela, with very useful information on preparation for a pilgrimage and

the meaning of pilgrimage, whether to Santiago de Compostela or any other pilgrimage journey.

www.santiago.ca
Web site of the Little Company of Pilgrims Canada (the Canadian Friends of the Way of St. James).

www.ricksteves.com
You may recognize Rick Steve's name from his numerous travel guides or his popular PBS show. His Web site is not to be missed. In particular, see the following:

- •www.ricksteves.com/plan/tips/home.htm
  (a wealth of useful travel tips)

- • www.ricksteves.com/plan/festivals/home.htm
  (an up-to-date list of festivals, many of them religious feasts, throughout Europe)

Selected Bibliography

Archdiocese of Oklahoma City. *Pilgrimage Passport: Jubilee 2000*. Oklahoma City: Archdiocese of Oklahoma City, 2000.

Archdiocese of Santa Fe. "El Santuario de Chimayo, the Lourdes of America." http://www.archdiocesesantafe.org/AboutASF/Chimayo.html. 2004.

Awakenings. "The Chartres Labyrinth." http://www.lessons4 living.com/chartres_labyrinth.htm. 2004.

Bacovcin, Helen, trans. *The Way of a Pilgrim and The Pilgrim Continues His Way: A New Translation*. Garden City, N.Y.: Image Books, 1978.

Barish, Eileen. *Lodging in Italy's Monasteries: Inexpensive Accommodations, Remarkable Historic Buildings, Unforgettable Settings*. Scottsdale, Ariz.: Anacapa Press, 2000.

———. *Lodging in Spain's Monasteries: Inexpensive Accommodations, Remarkable Historic Buildings, Memorable Settings*. Scottsdale, Ariz.: Anacapa Press, 2002.

Basilica of the National Shrine of the Immaculate Conception. "Our Lady of Hostyn Chapel." http://www.national shrineinteractive.com/Home/Home.cfm?ID=805&c =5&Type=s. 2004.

Bernes, Abbe G., Georges Veron, and L. Laborde Balen. *The Pilgrim Route to Compostela: In Search of St. James: A Practical Guide for Pilgrims and Walkers in Spain*. London: Robertson McCarta, 1990.

Bershad, David, and Carolina Mangone. *The Christian Travelers Guide to Italy*. Grand Rapids, Mich.: Zondervan, 2001.

Biallas, Leonard J. *Pilgrim: A Spirituality of Travel*. Quincy, Ill.: Franciscan Press, 2002.

Cameron, Julia. *The Artist's Way: A Spiritual Path to Higher Creativity*. New York: Tarcher, 1992.

———. *Blessings: Prayers and Declarations for a Heartful Life*. New York: Tarcher, 1998.

Cavins, Jeff, and Matthew Pinto. *Amazing Grace for Those Who Suffer: 10 Life-Changing Stories of Hope and Healing*. West Chester, PA: Ascension Press, 2002.

Chimayó. "Chimayó Today." http://www.chimayo.org/today.html .2004.

Coelho, Paulo. *The Pilgrimage: A Contemporary Quest for Ancient Wisdom*. Translated by Alan Clarke. San Francisco: HarperSanFrancisco, 1995. Reprint, San Francisco: Harper-SanFrancisco, 2000.

Copp, Jay. *The Liguori Guide to Catholic U.S.A.: A Treasury of Churches, Schools, Monuments, Shrines, and Monasteries*. Liguori, Mo.: Liguori, 1999.

Cousineau, Phil. *The Art of Pilgrimage: The Seeker's Guide to Making Travel Sacred*. Berkeley, Calif.: Conari Press, 1998.

Currie, Jim. *The Mindful Traveler: A Guide to Journaling and Transformative Travel*. Chicago: Open Court, 2000.

Davies, Bethan, and Ben Cole. *Walking the Camino de Santiago*. Vancouver, Canada: Pili Pala Press, 2003.

De Caussade, Jean-Pierre. *Abandonment to Divine Providence*. Translated by John Beevers. Garden City, NY: Image, 1975.

Dillard, Annie. *Teaching a Stone to Talk: Expeditions and Encounters*. New York: HarperCollins, 1982.

Dispenza, Joseph. *The Way of the Traveler: Making Every Trip a Journey of Self-Discovery*. Santa Fe, NM: John Muir, 1999. Reprint, Emeryville, CA: Avalon Travel, 2001.

Fátima Sanctuary. "The Apparitions." http://www .santuariofatima.pt/indexeng.htm. 2004.

Frey, Nancy Louise. *Pilgrim Stories: On and off the Road to Santiago*. Berkeley: University of California Press, 1998.

García-Monge, José Antonio, and Juan Antonio Torres Prieto. *Camino de Santiago: Viaje al interior de uno mismo*. Caminos series. Bilbao, Spain: Desclée de Brouwer, 1999.

Gitlitz, David M., and Linda Kay Davidson. *The Pilgrimage Road to Santiago: The Complete Cultural Handbook*. New York: St. Martin's Griffin, 2000.

Grodi, Marcus C. *Journeys Home*. Santa Barbara, Calif.: Queen-ship, 1997.

Groody, Daniel G. *Border of Death, Valley of Life: An Immigrant Journey of Heart and Spirit*. Lanham, Md.: Rowman & Little-field, 2002.

Hume, Basil. *To Be a Pilgrim: A Spiritual Notebook*. London: St. Paul, 1984.

Kidd, Sue Monk. *When the Heart Waits: Spiritual Direction for Life's Sacred Questions*. San Francisco: Harper & Row, 1990.

Kimmelman, Michael. "Out of the Deep," *The New York Times Magazine*. October 13, 2002.

Mandelker, Amy, and Elizabeth Powers, eds. *Pilgrim Souls: An Anthology of Spiritual Autobiographies*. New York: Simon & Schuster, 1999.

The Mary Page. "The Grotto of Unyang, Pusan, South Korea." http://www.udayton.edu/mary/resources/shrines/grotto/grottoof.html. 2003.

Melczer, William, trans. *The Pilgrim's Guide to Santiago de Com-postela*. New York: Italica, 1993.

Monahan, David. *The Shepherd Cannot Run: Letters of Stanley Rother, Missionary and Martyr*. Oklahoma City: Archdiocese of Oklahoma City, 1984.

Muller, Wayne. *Legacy of the Heart: The Spiritual Advantages of a Painful Childhood*. New York: Fireside, 1992.

Murphy-O'Connor, Jerome. *The Holy Land: An Oxford Ar-chaeological Guide from Earliest Times to 1700*. Oxford Archaeological Guides series. Oxford: Oxford University Press, 1998.

National Cowboy & Western Heritage Museum. "End of the Trail." http://www.cowboyhalloffame.org/g_trai.html. 2004.

Nhat Hanh, Thich. *The Miracle of Mindfulness: A Manual on Meditation*. Translated by Mobi Ho. Boston: Beacon Press, 1976.

Norris, Kathleen. *The Quotidian Mysteries: Laundry, Liturgy, and "Women's Work."* New York: Paulist Press, 1998.

Nouwen, Henri J. M. *Life of the Beloved: Spiritual Living in a Secular World*. New York: Crossroad, 1992.

———. *The Inner Voice of Love: A Journey through Anguish to Freedom*. New York: Doubleday, 1996.

———. *Here and Now: Living in the Spirit*. New York: Crossroad, 1994.

———. *The Return of the Prodigal Son: A Story of Homecoming*. New York: Doubleday, 1992.

Oben, Freda Mary. *Edith Stein: Scholar, Feminist, Saint*. New York: Alba House, 1988.

O'Reilly, Sean, and James O'Reilly, eds. *Pilgrimage: Adventures of the Spirit*. San Francisco: Travelers' Tales, 2000.

Puhl, Louis J., trans. *The Spiritual Exercises of St. Ignatius: Based on Studies in the Language of the Autograph*. Vintage Spiritual Classics series. New York: Vintage, 2000.

Raju, Alison. *The Way of St. James: Le Puy to Santiago, a Walker's Guide*. Milnthorpe, U.K. Cicerone, 1999.

Saint-Joseph's Oratory of Mount Royal. "The Founder: Brother André." http://www.saint-joseph.org/dynamic/section/brAndre/index.asp?Language=En. 2004.

Sanctuary Our Lady of Lourdes. "The Encounters with the Blessed Virgin Mary." http://www.lourdes-france.org/index.php?goto_centre=ru&contexte=en&id=417&id_rubrique=413. 2004.

Scaperlanda, María Ruiz. *The Seeker's Guide to Mary*. Chicago: Loyola Press, 2002.

———. *Edith Stein: St. Teresa Benedicta of the Cross*. Huntington, IN: Our Sunday Visitor, 2001

———. *Their Faith Has Touched Us: The Legacies of Three Young Oklahoma City Bombing Victims*. Kansas City, MO: Sheed & Ward, 1997.

———. "From Ashes to Easter: From the Dying Desert of Our Dying Marriage We Gave Birth to Hope," *The Lutheran* http://www.thelutheran.org/9704/page16.html, online reprint (April 1997).